MW00338921

Searching for
FLEMISH (BELGIAN)
Ancestors

JOZEF J. GOETHALS
In collaboration with
Karel Denys, CICM

CLEARFIELD

Copyright © 2007
by Jozef J. Goethals
All Rights Reserved.

Printed for
Clearfield Company by
Genealogical Publishing Co.
Baltimore, Maryland
2007

Library of Congress Control Number 2007922875

ISBN-13: 978-0-8063-5342-5
ISBN-10: 0-8063-5342-2

Made in the United States of America

CONTENTS

There are excellent "how to" books for genealogical research teaching you solid genealogical research methods and guiding you through the array of sources to be explored. For Americans of Flemish ancestry, whose knowledge of the Flemish language is waning, there is a need for a guide to help them descend into their Flemish family history.

An examination of guidebooks on genealogical research of European countries has convinced us that there is a need for the present publication. There are outstanding research manuals in Flemish showing the way through genealogical sources. Publications in English, however, treat Belgium only in a skeletal manner. Fr. Karel Denys, a life-long genealogy enthusiast and co-founder of the Genealogical Society of Flemish Americans, published a series of articles in the Flemish American Heritage magazine, filling, in part, this void. We decided that presenting our combined experiences to a wider American public would benefit the Flemish American researcher.

The main thrust of this work is to introduce you to the genealogical sources that are obtainable in the United States, i.e. sources that could save you a trip to the "old country", and to assist you in finding and interpreting these sources.

The introduction sketches the history of Flanders and Belgium and the waves of emigration to America. This basic information will allow you to place your ancestors in a historical context.

The first section describes some Belgian sources available in the United States which should be reviewed before your venture into the civil and parish records of Flanders: internet web sites, genealogical societies, library collections etc.

In the second and third sections you find a detailed analysis of the vital records of the civil Registry (1796-1900) and the Parish Registers (ca 1600-1796). Birth, marriage and death records are analyzed and translated from Flemish, French and Latin.

The fourth section introduces you to the history and content of other sources of the so-called *Ancien Régime* (Old Regime) before 1796: court records, orphan bench records, notary records, tax records, et al. These sources provide you with information which make the vital records come alive.

In the appendices we provide some practical research tools: among other things, an introduction to Flemish first names and surnames, state archives in Flanders, and a glossary of genealogy terms in Flemish, French and Latin.

Since the greatest number of emigrants to the United States originated from Flanders and our combined research experience concentrated on Flemish sources, the book is limited to the search for Flemish/Belgian ancestors, as the title suggests.

Throughout the work we have listed some "tips for the researcher" saving you frustration and time. They are introduced by the sign ᛞ.

A heartfelt word of thanks to Fr. Karel Denys who permitted the use of his published materials and whose advice is really appreciated. We also thank Joe Garonzik of the Genealogical Publishing Company, for his guidance and enthusiasm for this project. Thanks also go to Henry W. Goethals, my editor, for his generous and expert support.

We hope that this opuscule will assist you in finding your ancestors and will contribute to Belgian genealogy research in America. Good hunting!

Jozef Goethals, Baltimore, MD
In collaboration with Karel Denys C.I.C.M., Arlington, VA

Few Americans are aware that Belgium only emeerged as an independent nation in 1830. Located between The Netherlands, Germany, France and Luxembourg and approximately the same size as the State of Maryland, this small European nation has for centuries been the focal point of international power politics.

Belgium is a constitutional monarchy with a population of approximately 10,396,000. King Albert II, the current monarch, is the titulat head of state.Brussels, the capital city, is currently also the headquarters of the Europen Union. The federal government comprises three autonomous regions, namely, Flaners, which is Flemish-speaking; Wallonia, which is French-speaking; and Brabant, the capital region which includes the city of Brussels and which is bilingual in Flemish and French. The three regions are self-governing, comparable to the state system in the United States. Of three official languages, approximately six million Belgians speak Flemish, four million speak French and 70,000 speak German. The regions are made up of nine provinces. Four of these -- West Flanders, East Flanders, Antwerpen and Limburg-- are Flemish; four-- Hainaut, Namur. Liège and luxembourg-- are French (or Walloon), and one, Brabant, is partly Flemish and partly French.

Belgium

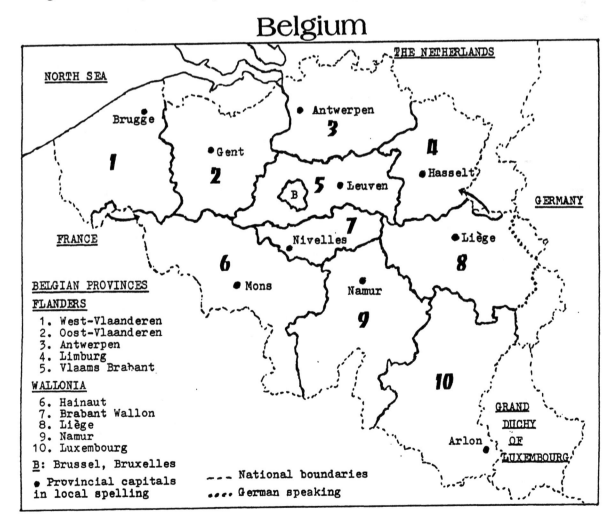

Over the centuries, the boundaries of the area often changed and the country adopted several names: *Flanders, the Low Countries, the Burgundian Netherlands, the Spanish Netherlands, the 17 Provinces, the Southern (present Belgium) and Northern Netherlands (present Holland), Belgium.*

Placing ancestors in an historical context is always important for a good family history. This is not only essential to understanding their daily lives, but it is critical in locating genealogical sources. One has to know under which administrative jurisdiction an ancestor was living: was he a vassal reporting to the lord of the manor? Was he a *poorter* (burgher) reporting to the local aldermen? Was he a citizen reporting to the civil administration?

A basic understanding of Flanders' history and governmental institutions is essential: this next section provides an overview of the history of Flanders and Belgium. In the ensuing sections the history and procedures of church and governmental institutions will be further developed.

The "Leo Belgicus" (Latin for "the Belgian Lion") is a cartographic depiction of the 17 provinces of the Netherlands, introduced by the Autrian cartographer Michael Aitsinger in 1583. The heraldic figure of the lion occured in many of the coats of arms of the provinces. The image of the Leo Belgicus became very popular and exists in many different designs. The above version was created by Pieter Van der Keere in Amsterdam in 1617.

Julius Caesar conquered the territory now called Belgium between 57 and 50 B.C. and made it one of the three provinces of Gaul. In his *De Bello Gallico* he praised the bravery of the Belgians ("horum omnium fortissimi sunt Belgae".) Roman civilization, however, did not exert a great impact on the area the Romans called *Gallia Belgica*. Toward the end of the third century the Franks, a Germanic tribe, immigrated into the fertile region between the rivers Seine and Rhine. The Frankish king Clovis (466-511) expanded his "Merovingian Kingdom", which included the present Flemish territory, to the south and the east. During the reign of Charlemagne (768-814) the Flemish territory sat at the center of the Frankish kingdom.

The name "Flanders" was first mentioned in the 8th century in the *Vita Eligii* (Life of Eligius), a bishop of Tournai around 640. It was called *pagus flandriensis* and denoted then the region around Brugge.

The first capital of the early Frankish kingdom was Tongeren, situated in today's Limburg Province. When the rulers extended their kingdom to the south, Tournai (Doornik) became the capital, and later Paris. Eventually, the Northern part of the kingdom became the "County of Flanders"

The Flemish Counts (863-1383)

After the end of the Viking attacks, the policies of 23 Flemish counts revived Flanders and made it into " an example of modernity, wealth and strength".[2] In 863, *Baldwin I*, who had married the daughter of the French King Charles II, became the first Count of Flanders. The county was bordered by the North Sea and stretched to the river Scheldt, with an area in the south (presently northern France), and another area in the north (presently Dutch Zeeland). This became the seed from which Flanders developed. *Baldwin II "the Bald"* (879-918) created peace and order, stimulating economic expansion. He had married the daughter of King Alfred the Great of England, and because of this English connection, encouraged the nascent cloth industry based on English wool.

Between 900 and 1000, the power of the Carolingian family waned while the feudal states, including Flanders, grew in importance. The counts of Flanders and the Dukes of Brabant remained strong militarily while fostering the development of cities and industry in their respective regions, with emphasis on the construction of canals and promotion of the linen industry. The less productive parts of the county were converted to meadowland for agricultural use. Monasteries and abbeys played an important role in development by establishing schools and teaching new agricultural methods. The monasteries also play a vital role in the rise of towns in Flanders. By the 11th century Flanders was a vassal of France by dint of its possessions west of the Scheldt River as

---

[1] For a more expanded study of Belgian history, see Bernard A. Cook, *Belgium. A History,* Peter Lang Publishing, 2002.

[2] Patricia Carson, *The Fair Face of Flanders,* Lannoo, Tielt, sixth printing, revised, 2001, p.33.

well as a vassal of the Holy Roamn Empire in that it had acquired property east of the Scheldt.

From the 12th to the 14th century, the counts forged international relationships by participating in the Crusades. Count *Robert II* was crowned "King of Jerusalem" in 1101 and *Baldwin IX* became the "Latin Emperor of Constantinople" in 1204. During that same period, Flanders became a great textile manufacturer, with wool imported from England and fabricated on Flemish looms. The growing class of merchants and craftsmen organized themselves into guilds for their mutual assistance. The counts, seeing an opportunity to strengthen their feudal jurisdiction, granted privileges to the cities, laying the foundation for the *Schepenbank* (Alderman's Bench) and in doing so, creating a degree of self-government in the cities. *Philip of Alsace* began granting privileges to the cities early in the 12th century. These privilege charters gave the cities power to manage their municipal government in financial, administrative and judicial matters. The *Keure* of Gent is a splendid example. This municipal government structure survived until the French occupation of Flanders in 1796.

The French kings always had a love-hate relationship with its powerful vassal to the North and they tried to make Flanders a French province. In 1300 Philip IV occupied Flanders. On 18 May 1302 the population of Brugge attacked and killed the French patricians in the town. (The "Matins of Brugge"). The Flemish organized an army of townsfolk and a number of mounted knights who were faithful to the Flemish count, and they confronted and defeated the French army in the *Battle of the Golden Spurs* on 11 July 1302 in Kortrijk under the leadership of Jan Breydel and Pieter de Coninck. Even today this victory is still seen as a symbol of Flemish independence. The war continued until 1305 when the Treaty of Athis-sur-Orge was signed, recognizing the "independence" of Flanders, even though the region remained under the control of the French crown.

The Burgundian Period (1383-1477)

On the death of *Louis of Male* in 1383, the last Flemish count, Burgundy acquired Flanders. In 1369, *Philip the Bold*, Duke of Burgundy, had married *Margaret of Flanders*, daughter of Louis of Male. The Duke took over the greater part of the Low Countries. He relocated his capital from Burgundy to his new rich county and relocated the powerful Council of Flanders from Lille (Rijsel) to Gent. The Burgundian dukes expanded their possessions with the addition of Namur, Brabant, Holland and Luxemburg, to what was known as the *XVII Provinces* or the *Lower Countries = Nether-lands*, of which Flanders was referred to as the *Southern Netherlands*. This area was often depicted as the "Leo Belgicus". (The Belgian Lion)

The era of the dukes of Burgundy is noted for its vast development of art and culture in the Burgundian Netherlands: the "Flemish Primitives" as the Van Eyck brothers, the tapestry weavers of Brussels, Doornik and Leuven, the Notre Dame cathedral of Antwerp and the city Hall of Brussels, the erection of the University of Leuven in 1425, and the foundation of the Golden Fleece.

The Habsburg Period

The era of the Burgundian counts ended with the marriage of *Mary of Burgundy* to *Maximilian of Austria,* member of the Habsburg family. When the latter became emperor of the Holy Roman Empire in 1493, he left the Netherlands to his son *Philip the Handsome.* Philip, who had married Joanna of Castile de Aragon in 1496, claimed the Spanish throne in 1504 and Flanders was now under the rule of the Spanish Habsburg dynasty and would remain there until 1713 when the Austrian House of Habsburg took over.

When Philip the Handsome died in 1506, his sister *Margarita of Austria* became the regent of Flanders until 1515. Philip's son Charles, born in Gent 24 February 1500 - living in Belgium's folklore as *" Keizer Karel" (Emperor Charles)* - became king of Spain in 1516 and inherited the Austrian territories and the Holy Roman Empire at the death of Maximilian in 1519. He ruled mostly from Madrid and left the government of the XVII Provinces to his aunt Margarita of Austria and his sister Marie of Hungary. He resigned from the throne in 1555 and gave the Spanish Netherlands to his son *Philip II.* The latter appointed his half-sister *Margareta of Parma* regent of the Netherlands.

In the meantime the Protestant Reformation was in full swing. The traditional faith had been partly undermined by Humanism. Many of the Flemish intelligentsia and merchants joined the reform movement and seized control of many cities. Several towns had their "protestant dictators' - like Gent in 1577-1584. The Flemish resented the high-handed treatment of the reformers by the Spanish. In 1565, the lower nobility, among whom were many Calvinists, formed the *Eedverbond der Edelen* (Compromise of the Nobles) who assumed the name of *Geuzen.* This marked the start of the *Beroerlijke Tijden* (Troubled Times) and the first iconoclastic destruction of churches in Flanders. Margarita of Parma returned to Spain in 1567 and Philip II sent *Alva* with thousands of soldiers to the Netherlands to put down the rebellion. A three-year "reign of terror" followed, during which Alva executed no less than 6,000 people and confiscated much property. .

After Alva left, Philip II appointed *Alexander Farnese*, Duke of Parma, as governor of the Netherlands. In a short time he succeeded in uniting the 10 southern Catholic provinces and giving them political freedom (present Belgium). The northern 7 Calvinist provinces (the present-day Netherlands) were united that same year. And so the Spanish Netherlands were split for good into a Catholic south and a Calvinist north: it would take the Spaniards until 1648 to approve this split.

In 1589 Philip II gave the Spanish Netherlands to his daughter *Isabella* (1566-1633) and her husband the Archduke *Albert of Austria.* During their reign the area enjoyed peace and prosperity and Flanders became a bulwark of the Counter Reformation. The Peace of Munster in 1648 ended the 80 Years War and Spain recognized the sovereignty of the XVII Provinces.

The Spanish dynasty ended with the death of Charles II in 1700. A war of succession broke out on Southern Netherlands territory. The Peace of Utrecht in 1713 awarded the Southern Netherlands to the Austrian emperor Charles VI, Flanders thus returning to Austrian Habsburg rule. During the reign of *Maria Theresia* (1740-1780) Flanders flourished economically and culturally. Maria Theresia expanded the road system, brought in new industries and founded the "Theresian colleges" in the spirit of the Enlightenment.

Under Maria Theresia's son *Joseph II* (1780-1790), the period of Theresian peace and prosperity came to an end. Joseph was a typical 18th century enlightened despot, not unlike Catherina in Russia and Frederick in Prussia. He remodeled the civil and tax administration, and the judiciary. He submitted religion to the authority of the state, regulated the liturgy, instituted civil marriage, abolished some monasteries, and replaced church seminaries with state seminaries. For all this, he earned the nickname *emperor sacristan.*

Starting in 1785, however, the opposition to Joseph grew. Two groups formed: the *Statists* under the leadership of Henri van der Noot wanted to return to the "Ancien Régime" and the privileges of the clergy, the nobility and the provinces. The *Vonckists,* under Jan-Frans Vonck wanted a more democratic state. The two parties organized themselves militarily and occupied the Netherlands in late 1789. On 10 January 1790 the States General declared the Independence of the *United States of Belgium,* with a new constitution based on the American Articles of Confederation. No other European powers recognized the new state. Leopold II reoccupied the Netherlands at the end of 1790. In 1794 the Netherlands were finally conquered by the French revolutionary armies, and in 1794 and 1795 were annexed to France. The country was divided into nine departments (still recognizable as Belgium's nine provinces). The French imposed their French civil administration and French language on the entire country. Napoleon added the Northern Netherlands in 1804.

Towards Belgian Independence

After the defeat of Napoleon in Waterloo in 1815, the Congress of Vienna created the United Kingdom of the Netherlands (today's Belgium and Holland) under *William I of Orange,* as a buffer against French power. William's rule survived only 15 years. The Southern Netherlands did not like the policies of Willem: the church hated his Protestantism and the liberals hated his despotic policies. On 25 August 1830 a second revolution broke out in Brussels. In less than two months the Dutch garrisons were expelled from the territory, and an independent state was declared on *4 October 1830.* The nine provinces of the Southern Netherlands were now a single state: *Belgium.* The provinces chose "constitutional monarchy" as their form of government. Leopold of Saxe-Coburg, widower of princess Charlotte, the daughter of king George IV of England, and uncle of Queen Victoria, became the first monarch of the new Belgium on 21 July 1831.

The Frankish Kingdom	Carolingian Period 768-863	*The Holy Roman Empire*
The County of Flanders	The Flemish Counts 863-1384	
	Burgundian Netherlands 1384-1477	
	Seventeen Provinces 1477-1556	
	Spanish Netheerlands 1556-1581	
The United provinces	- The Southern Netherlands	

	1581-1713	
1581-1795	- The Austrian Netherlands	
	1713-1794	
	The First French Republic	
	1795-1805	
	The First French Empire	
	1805-1815	
	The United Kingdom of the Netherlands	
	1815-1830	
The Netherlands	Constitutional Monarchy Belgium	*Luxemburg*
	1830	

French versus Flemish: a Linguistic and Cultural War

From the annexation of Flanders in 1795, French became the official language of the country although the majority of the population was Flemish-speaking. Until well into the 20th, the French speaking minority banned Flemish in all schools and universities and in all dealings with the civil administration. A growing self esteem and pride in the Flemish language led to an increasing presence of Flemish in public life towards the end of the 19th century. After arduous battles, Flemish was finally reintroduced in schools and universities in the 1930s. It had been more than a linguistic struggle: it was the tip of the iceberg of political, social, cultural and economic apartheid policies. Speaking Flemish was seen as "uncultured" : the archbishop of Belgium stated in the 1920s that Flemish "is unfit as a vehicle for religious, cultural and artistic values." The language struggle reflects a desire for the emancipation of the Flemish majority against the French-speaking minority in all levels of public life.This struggle has led to the federalization of the Belgian state into Flemish, French and bilingual Brussels regions at the end of the 20th century (see above).

As a visitor to Belgium, always be aware of their "language sensitivity": as known polyglots the Flemish will easily communicate in English and will not mind if you order one of their famous waffles in English. You might get a frown, however, if you try your French on them. In Bastogne you might be ignored if you try your Flemish...

"Dutch" and "Flemish"

Most Americans are unaware that Dutch (often called "Hollandish" - *Hollands*) and Flemish (*Vlaams*) are only one language. The official Dutch-Flemish language, in its written form, is the same in Flanders and the Netherlands, although its pronuntiation may differ. To understand these differences, one could consider the differences between American and British English.

There is a rich variety of dialects, differing in vocabulary and pronunciation from province to province and often from city to city, which often requires people from different parts of the country to speak "official" Flemish in order to be understood.

❦ ❦ ❦

THE EMIGRATION FROM BELGIUM TO AMERICA

Belgian emigration to America began in earnest only in the last quarter of the 19th century. Two centuries earlier, the West Indian Company in the Spanish Netherlands equipped a vessel, the Nieu Netherlandt, to sail to the New World. A Fleming, William Usselinx, founder of the West Indian Company, took a group of 30 Protestant families, mostly Walloons, to Manhatten in 1624. It was *Peter Minuit*, the director general of New Netherland, who secured the title to the whole Manhatten Island for the purported sum of $ 24.00. Minuit, coming from Wesel, Westphalia, Germany, is said to be of Belgian parentage and knew Flemish and French. In 1630 Staten Island was bought in about the same way as was Manhatten, and Hoboken, named after a village near Antwerpen, followed soon after.

These early Belgian settlers were followed later by Catholics as the church sent Catholic priests to the new colony. The most famous of these priests was *Father Louis Hennepin*, born in Ath, Hainaut. As a chaplain, he accompanied La Salle in 1675, sailing to Frontenac. He traveled the northern territories extensively and is said to have been the first European to describe the Niagara Falls in his journal. During the next 100 years, only small numbers of Belgians emigrated to America.

This would soon change because of the economic and social circumstances in the "Old World". As a result of the industrial revolution and a demographic explosion, many rural laborers were out of work and had to seek their livelihood outside the borders of Belgium- first in neighboring countries, and soon accross the ocean. Belgian emigration to the the United States begins about halfway in the 19th century and ends a good one hundred years later. Flemings and Walloons, mainly farmers, settle in the American Midwest. The reasons for this Belgian migration are to be found on both sides of the Atlantic ocean.

In the 19th and early 20th century, two forces, on both sides of the Atlantic, precipitated the emigration from Flanders to the United States.

On the European side, the poverty of Flanders, caused by a population explosion and socio-economic problems, compelled many to try their luck across the Atlantic. In America, the need for farmers and laborers and the promise of land made it the "promised land" where every one could achieve the "American Dream".

In the middle of the 19th century, the population of Flanders started to explode and the country would double its population from 4.3 million to 8.5 million by 1947.

The larger part of the Flemish population depended on their farms for their livelihood. The rapid fragmentation of farms, caused by the growth of families, resulted in a surplus of agrarian laborers. Some farms were reduced to 0.5 hectares (1.5 acres), unable to sustain the families, reducing them to poverty. The highest poverty rate was in West- and East-Flanders and some parts of Brabant.

At the same time, Flanders witnessed the demise of its textile industry. Textile production was based on a thriving domestic spinning and weaving industry.The primary and secondary incomes of most working people were derived from this household industry and for most farmers it was a necessary second income. Around 1830 there were an estimated 220,000 spinners (not counting the children) and 57,000 weavers in East and West Flanders, out of population of 850,000. In 1834 England began mechanizing the weaving industry and exported cheaper linen to the continent. France lowered its import duties in 1836, and the Flemish export to France was cut in half: 50 % of the house industry workers lost their lievelihood. Poverty became rampant, and in a few years public assistance grew from 18 percent in 1837 to 24 percent in 1844. The city of Gent supported 32.5 percent of its population with public assistance.

This economic disaster was aggravated by the 1845 potato disease and wheat pest. An extremely virulent mold attacked the potato harvest, first in Belgium and Holland, and subsequently all over Europe. Agricultural losses were estimated at 1/4 to 1/2 of the harvest. In West and East Flanders the potato harvest declined by 90 %. To make matters worse, typhoid and cholera epidemics broke out and claimed scores of lives: 28,000 victims fell in 1848 alone. The combination of the demise of the domestic textile industry, the surplus of agrarian workers, the disastrous consequences of the potato disease, and the epidemics created the need to emigrate.

In the fourteen years after the Independence of Belgium (1830), around 30,000 Belgians emigrated to neighboring countries and one out of ten left Europe.

Before 1840 only a few Belgians emigrated to "America" - as the United States was called in Belgium. When bands of destitute people and vagrants were placed in "beggar colonies" in some of the cities in Flanders, the government saw a chance to solve a problem. The Council of the Province of Antwerpen encouraged these people to emigrate to the United States and they even paid their transatlantic trip - costing the province less than the public assistance they would otherwise have to provide. Other provinces followed suit, but after the transportation of an estimated 630 of these vagrants, paupers and beggars - including ex-prisoners- by 1856 the United States terminated the influx and the Belgian government limited its direct involvement to advertizing and the protection of emigrants.

During the 1850s however, thousands of farmers emigrated to Wisconsin, where Green Bay became the largest Belgian settlement in the United States. Many of them were "recruited" by the positive reports they received from family and friends. A Belgian from Wisconsin writes in 1850: "In America it is easy to save money, there is better food, there is no military service, the taxes are lower, there is equality between employer and employee, and the manner of living is simpler and healthier". [3] The two decades 1861-1880 brought another 14,000 Belgians to American shores.

In 1880s we witness the beginning of a real upswing in the immigration from Belgium. In Belgium, the agricultural sector had another serious set-back and almost 100,000 farmers quit their trade. Between 1880 and 1890, more than 20,000 emigrate to the United States. The next four decades tens of thousands follow: between 1881 and 1930 ca 109,000 Belgians are recorded as

[3] Dirk Musschoot, *We gaan naar Amerika, Vlaamse Landverhuizers naar de Nieuwe Wereld,* Lannoo, Tielt 2002, 31.

immigrants in America, reaching an all time high of 41,365 between the pre-World War II years of 1901-1910. More than two thirds of the immigrants were Flemish - mostly from the provinces of East and West-Flanders - and 25 % were from Wallonia.

During this immigration wave, industrial workers outnumbered farmers. Many Flemish immigrants headed for Moline, Illinois and for Detroit. Groups of Flemish farmers settled in Minnesota, where they established a large Flemish colony in Ghent in Lyon County. [4]

After the First World War, there is another influx of Belgian immigrants (1920: 6,574) but soon the restrictions imposed on immigration in 1920 and the depression of the 1930s reduce the number to a trickle.

In the years after the Second World War only a small number of Flemings immigrate, although Robert Houtave claims there was "mini-wave" in 1951-1960 with an influx of 18,575. [5]

Today, Flemish immigrants work in international business, banks, world organizations and educational institutions, and only a few settle here permanently and become American citizens. The United States census of 1980 records 360,277 people of Belgian ancestry. The greatest concentration is found in the Upper Midwest: 31 % live in the states of Michigan and Wisconsin.

---

[4] An excellent history of that colony is Robert Houtave, *Flandria Americana, Ghent, Minnesota. Een studie van Vlaamse Emigranten naar het Amerikaanse Continent*, Flandria Nostra, Torhout 1985.
[5] Robert Houtave, *Flandria Americana*, 10.

The sculpture " The Flemish Emigrant" is the brain child of Ludwig Vandenbussche, representative of the *Gazette van Detroit* in Flanders. Ludwig and his wife Doreen are residents of Leke-Diksmuide in West-Flanders and have many family members in Canada and the U.S.A.. Ludwig became interested in Flemish emigration in 1979 and has been involved since with anything that has to do with Flemish emigration to North America.

In 2001 he was instrumental in the creation of the "Canadian Square" and the "Canadian Liberation Monument" in Leke-Diksmuide in honor of the British Columbia Regiment which liberated the town from German occupation on 7 September 1944. The monument was created by a local artist Patrick Steen.

DE VLAAMSE EMIGRANT

THE FLEMISH EMIGRANT

2004-2005

P. Steen - Leke - Belgium

At the beginning of 2001 Ludwig came up with the idea of creating a piece of art that would celebrate and memorialize the Flemish emigration to North America. With the assistance of the Belgian Canadian Consul, Mr. Frank Carruet, the provinical government of West-Flanders was approached to finance the project, but governmental help never materialized.

Ludwig and his wife Doreen decided to look for private sponsors for the project and raised the needed 12,500 Euros by September 2004. They commisioned Patrick Steen to create the sculpture.

On Sunday 26 September 2004, on the 90th anniversary of the *Gazette van Detroit*, the sculpture "The Flemish Emigrant" was presented to the press in Leke-Diksmuide. The work was flown to Andrews Air Force Base by the Belgian Air Force and shipped by truck to Delhi, Ontario. The striking statue represents a Flemish household waiting at the Rijnkaai in Antwerp to board a Red Star Line ship. The family is gazing at a North American skyline across a pool of water.

It was decided that the home of the art work would be Delhi, Ontario in Cananda, the only place in North America where Flemish language and culture are still flourishing. The very active *Belgian Club* in Delhi is the present host of the sculpture, but the local Tobacco and Heritage Museum has agreed to place the work in its permanent collection in case the Belgian Club ceases to exist.

Thanks to Ludwig and Doreen Vandenbussche, "The Flemish Emigrant" will be a permanent reminder of the many Flemish people who came to America to start a new life!

I. BELGIAN SOURCES IN THE U.S.A.

GENERAL SOURCES AND INTERNET WEBSITES

It is not wise to start looking for sources of the "old regime" before you collect all possible information available in the United States. Your search for ancestors in Belgium should only begin when you have found the location in Flanders from which your ancestors originated. and when they emigrated to America. So begin with your county courthouse where you will find registration of births, marriages, divorces, deaths; probate records, declarations of intention, petitions for naturalization, oaths of allegiance, land records etc. Local newspaper archives contain obituaries with lots of information on families. These news papers are in many cases available on microfilm in your local county library.

Pay a visit to your local FAMILY HISTORY CENTER of the Mormon Church: they have huge data bases, such as the IGI (International Genealogical Index). Their staffs are extremely cooperative and may help you locate previous research on your family surname. At the same time, get familiar with their procedures on how to order microfilms on ancient Belgian records.

If you have access to the internet, a lot of sources are at your finger tips! [6] A first "beginners source" is the SOCIAL SECURITY DEATH INDEX (SSDI) which can be freely accessed at < **www.search.ancestry.com/ssdi** > or at your local Family History Center where they usually have a CD-rom with these records. The records run from 1960.

Recently the records of ELLIS ISLAND have become available to the general public on the Internet. These records cover the period of 1892-1924 and show the arrivals at the immigration center.(< **http:// Ellisisland.org**>) For the period before Ellis Island, search the website < **www.castlegarden.org**> where you will find arrivals in New York 1830-1892.

The US FEDERAL CENSUS records (ten year periods) are an important source for the period 1850 to the recently available 1930 census (the data of the 1890 census were destroyed). For access to census records on line, go to < **www.census-online.com**> or <**www.censusfinder.com**> These websites can guide you to your state and even your county.

A visit to CYNDI'SLIST OF GENEALOGICAL SITES (< **http://www.Cyndyslist.com**>) is a must. Look under "Belgium" and this site will give you rich sources of Belgian information: general resource sites, history and culture of Belgium, mailing lists, societies, government and cities, libraries, archives, records, etc.

---

[6] A recently published work by William Dollarhide will be of great help to get you started : William Dollarhide, *Getting Started in Genealogy Online,* Genealogical Publishing Co., Baltimore MD 2006.

Another required site is the BELGIUM-ROOTS PROJECT,(< **http://belgium.rootsweb.com** >) hosted by Roots Web and recently owned and operated by Ancestry.Inc..Their mission statement, by their founder George Picavet, states:" Belgium Roots was created in July 1995 for the purpose of assisting the descendants of Belgian emigrants/immigrants living abroad in tracing their Belgian roots and exploring their Belgian heritage. There are no direct or indirect obligations, financial or otherwise, except for the total and unconditional respect for the personalities and the opinions of all participants." This website will guide you to a host of basic information on Belgium and serve as a portal to your search.

BELGIAN GENEALOGICAL SOCIETIES

The Genealogical Society of Flemish Americans (GSFA)

GSFA was founded in 1976, inspired by Michel Mispelon, president of the VVF (Flemish Association of Family History) during a visit to the Detroit area. He encouraged a group of about 20 people in Detroit to complete the data the Flemish association in Belgium already had on early emigrants. They began collecting more death memorial cards of friends and relatives and became acquainted with sources in the Detroit area. In 1977, Leon Buyse, the unofficial historian of "Belgians in America" [7] moved his extensive collection of Belgian-American records into the Fr. Taillieu residence and the GSFA center was born.

This center has a well-organized reference library with myriad information on Flemish genealogy: family histories, census records of a series of towns in Belgium, over 14,000 death memorial cards and 6,000 bereavement letters. Besides microfilms of the Flemish publications *De Volkstem (DepereWI) 1891-1919* and *Gazette van Moline (IL) 1907-1940*, they have made microfilms of the Flemish-English weekly newspaper *Gazette van Detroit (MI)* 1916-1986 and keep copies of this paper since 1987.

A $ 15.00 memberships fee to the association will give you its *Flemish American Heritage* magazine which GSFA publishes since 1983. (18740 Thirteen Mile Road, Roseville, MI 48066 ; tel (810) 776-9579.) Their website is sponsored by Roots.Web < **http://www.rootsweb.com/~gsfa** >.

---

[7] Philemon D. Sabbe and Leon Buyse, *Belgians in America,* Lannoo, Tielt (Belgium) 1960.

The Belgian Researchers

The *Belgian American Heritage Association* was founded in 1976 to provide information about Belgian ancestry, history and cultural heritage. The association has a Yahoo! group for members at < http:// groups.yahoo.com/group/The Belgian Researchers/ > .

Its quarterly magazine *Belgian Laces*, published in English " specializes in history-genealogy-heraldry, doing research for Belgians in the states and for Belgian Americans in Belgium." Membership dues are $ 12.00, which includes the magazine. They can be reached at 62073 Fruitdale Lane, La Grande OR 97850-5312; Tel (541) 963-6697; Fax: (541) 962-7604.

Next to articles on Belgian heritage and history, the magazine publishes lists of obits and naturalization records and features newly published books on genealogical and cultural subjects. Although they have some information on Flemish immigrants, the bulk of their information centers around the French-speaking section of Belgium.

PERIODICAL POST MAIL
Paid Roseville, Michigan

ONE YEAR SUBSCRIPTION IN US DOLLARS

USA $25   Canada $30   Belgium $50   Single Copy $1.00

Gazette van Detroit
SINDS 1914

The only Belgian newspaper in America serving the Belgian communities around the world for 92 years.

Vol. 92 No. 24   Belgian Publishing Co., Inc. • 18740 E. 13 Mile Rd. • Roseville, MI 48066-1378   November 23, 2006

| To contact us: gazettevandetroit @yahoo.com | BELGIAN BAND CELEBRATES 75 YEARS! *See page 5* | *See page 11* | "Uncle Pierre" on food shopping *See page 17* |

THE GAZETTE VAN DETROIT

The "Gazette van Detroit" is an important source of information for Belgians residing in the United States and Canada. Established in 1914 in Detroit, this newspaper is published bi-weekly in both English and Flemish and provides a vital link between Americans and Canadians of Flemish ancestry and relatives in Belgium.

The newspaper carries news items scanned from Belgian sources as well as news about Belgian clubs and organizations, principally in Illinois and Michigan. It prints death notices of noted Flemish Americans, genealogical reports, and the impressions of immigrants in their new country and their visits to the mother country, as well as recipes, feature stories and related items that help keep Flemish heritage alive in America.

As in many other ethnic communities, the Belgians created their own "press" in areas where Flemish influence was strong. The *Pere Standaard* and *De Volksstem* in Wisconsin were early examples.[8] At the start of the 20th century, the largest settlement of Flemings in America was in Moline, Illinois. The "Gazette van Moline" started publication in 1907, continuing until 1940. Meanwhile, growth of the automotive industry was attracting a large number of Flemish workers to Detroit. By 1913 Detroit had the largest Belgian colony in America.

Camille Cools, an immigrant from Moorslede (West-Flanders) was a correspondent for the Gazette van Moline from 1908-1911in the Detroit area. As an active defender and promotor of Flemish culture, he reported on - and to- the Flemish immigrants and helped them retain their heritage by making Flemish books available. On 14 August 1914, just after the outbreak of World War I, he published the first issue of the *Gazette van Detroit*. In an editorial he explained one of the main reasons for the publication:"... we cannot fail to inform our friends, who are not too familiar yet with the English language, about everything concerning the war in Europe..." (GVD, 13 Aug 1914, p.1) The paper not only reported on war events Europe but also on sports and other major events. The weekly paper, published exclusively in Flemish, was sold for 3 cents with a $1 cost for a yearly subscription. The initiative was a success, and by 1916 the paper had 20 correspondents in the U.S. , Canada and Belgium. Although initially focusing on the Detroit area, the paper gradually covered other areas of the country.

In 1940 the Gazette absorbed the *Gazette van Moline* and became "the only Belgian newspaper in America." By 1974, however, dwindling subscription led to the publication of the Gazette van Detroit in both English and Flemish in order to attract the growing number of immigrants who no longer read Flemish. The paper was also owned by the newly created non-profit *Belgian Publishing Co.* and moved its headquarters and archives to the Father Taillieu Residence in Roseville, Michigan.[9] In 1993 the paper switched to a bi-weekly publication.

In February 2006 the growing number of aging subscribers and second- and third-generation "Americanized" Flemings with a greatly reduced knowledge of the Flemish language created a critical situation for the paper, putting it on virtual "life support" and creating fears that it would not reach its 100th anniversary as a publication. Howeveer, Ludwig Vandenbussche, a correspondent for the Gazette in Belgium for 27 years. started a media campaign in Belgium " to save the only Belgian newspaper in America." The response was surprising. Ludwig initiated a campaign " 1000 Flemings x 10 Euro" which resulted in a flood of Euros. At the same time the Flemish government was contacted and allocated a subsidy to the project. On the American side, an expatriate, Leen De Doncker of Michigan, got interested in the Gazette and added new collaborators to the aging staff. In no time they changed its format, modernized the paper, and are developing a website. Today, the paper has taken off its life support system and seems well on its way to its 100th birthday in 2014.

A subscription costs $25 for USA, $ 30 for Canada and can be obtained from: Belgian Publishing Co.Inc., 18740 E. 13 Mile Road, Roseville MI 48066-1378. Their e-mail contact is **gazettevandetroit@yahoo.com**

---

[8] See Aranka Callens. *The cultural heritage through Flemish Immigration: A Comparative Study of the Gazette van Detroit between May 28, 1981-May 27, 1981 and January 9, 2003- November 13,2003.* VVF Afdeling Tielt, 31 Oktober 2004

[9] After its editor Leon Buyse passed away in 1982, Fr. Charles Denys, my collaborator for this work, became editor-in-chief of the paper until 1996.

The Belgian custom of death memorial cards originated around 1790. These cards were distributed during the funeral service and contain basic data about the birth and death of the deceased. At first they were handwritten and it wasn't until the 19th century that they were printed. In Flanders there are incredible collections of these cards preserved in archives and VVF documentation centers: the city library of Kortrijk (*stadsbiblioteek*) has a collection of more than one million of these cards.

Although not an American custom, the Belgian communities in America continued printing these memorial cards. Next to the 15,000 collected by the members of GSFA in Roseville, a monumental work of 14 volumes of death memorials cards by Paul Callens is of special interest. This author specializes in everything connected to Belgian emigration to the U.S.A. and Canada. The series began in January 2000 (Vol I); it's latest volume (XIV) was published April 2005 - and more volumes are coming. Each volume contains ca 1,000 death memorial cards and newspaper clippings, not only of Belgians deceased in the U.S.A. but also of Belgian immigrants who went back to their motherland to die, or even those who spent only some years in America. The oldest card is from 1879.

Another important source for "beginners" is the same author's *Amerikaanse Zantingen - (American Gleanings)*: a two volume work which the author coins as "a road to sources about America." It is a list of Flemish and English publications from which he "gleaned" all information relevant to Belgian emigration-immigration.

Copies of these two works are available at the following libraries or genealogical societies:

Belgian American Texas Club, San Antonio, Texas
Burton Historical Collection of the Detroit Public Library, Detroit, Michigan
Center for Belgian Culture of Western Illinois, Moline, Illinois
Chattam Genealogical Society, Chattam Public Library, Ontario
Chilliwac Museum, BC, Canada
Family History Library, Salt Lake City, Utah
Genealogical Society of Flemish Americans, Roseville, Michigan
Harvard College Library, Cambridge, Massachusetts
Hoboken Museum, Hoboken, New York
Johnson County Genealogical Society, Shawnee, Kansas
Library of Congress, Washington D.C.
Oakland County Genealogical Society, Bermingham, Michigan
St. Joseph County Public Library, South Bend, Indiana
South Carolina Library, University of South Carlina, Columbia, South Carolina
State Historical Society of Wisconsin, Madison, Wisconsin
The Belgian Researchers, Peru, Indiana
The National Library of Canada, Ottowa, Canada

The Newberry Library, Chicago, Illinois
The New York Genealogical and Biographical Society, New York, New York

✠
BID VOOR DE ZIEL
van Zaliger

Barbara De Backere

Echtgenoote van

Julius Teerlinck

geboren te Moerbeke. Belgie, 28 December 1856, godvruchtig overleden te Ghent. Minn., 9 Januari 1916, versterkt door de laatste HH. Sacramenten.

Zij was lid der Altaarvereeniging en van het Apostelschap des Gebeds.

Zij was eene goede en zoetaardige vrouw; haar rondborstig karakter en aangename omgang wonnen haar de achting en genegenheid van iedereen.
H. Aug.

Zij heeft de pijnen eener smertelijke ziekelijkheid met voorbeeldig geduld verdregen.— Hoe gelukkig en voorzichtig is hij die binst het leven tracht te zijn gelijk hij geern zou gevonden worden in de dood. Thom. a Kemp.

Welbeminde Echtgenoot en Zoon, ik sterf maar mijne liefde voor u sterft niet. Vaart wel! tot wederziens in het Hemelsch Vaderland.

Zoet Hert van Jesus, wees mijne liefde! (300 dag. afl.)
R. I. P.

GAZETTE VAN MOLINE MOLINE, ILL.

Pray for the Soul of ✠ Bidt voor de Ziel van

Maurice B. De Paepe

husband of   echtgenoot van
ANNA NORMAN

Born in Belgium, December 22, 1895. Died at Rock Island, Illinois, June 6, 1955. Fortified by the last Holy Sacraments.

"We have loved him during life, let us not abandon him, until we have conducted him by our prayers into the house of the Lord."

The suffering of illness adds a new lustre to the crown which God has prepared for us in heaven. He who dies in submission to His divine Will, dies a holy death. St. Al.

Merciful Jesus, grant him eternal rest.

Geboren in Belgie, den 22 Dec. 1895. Overleden te Rock Island, Illinois, den 6 Juni, 1955. Voorzien der laatste Heilige Sakramenten.

Wij hebben hem bemind op aarde. Laat ons hem niet vergeten, totdat onze gebeden hem gebracht hebben in het huis des Heeren. H. Abr.

Bermhertige Jesus, geeft hem de eeuwige rust. (100 d. afl.)

MODEL PRINTERS. MOLINE. ILL.

IN MEMORY
of

DANIEL DENEVE
beloved husband of GABRIELLE
born in Olsene, Belgium, Dec. 18, 1900;
died in Needles, California,
November 11, 1941.

and of

GABRIELLE DENEVE
(born ROELANDTS)
beloved wife of DANIEL
born in Bruges, Belgium. Jan. 14, 1905;
died in Needles, California,
November 11, 1941.

Above are some examples of death memorial cards
(From Paul Callens, Death Memorial Cards, with permission)

II. CIVIL RECORDS IN FLANDERS FROM 1796

On the 20th of April 1792 France declared war on Austria and invaded Flanders, then under Austrian rule. On 17 June 1796, in full control of the country, the French imposed civil law on Flanders.

The French introduced a new administrative system centered on the municipalities. The municipal authorities were charged with recording all vital records in an array of adminstrative enteties: the Civil Registry (births, marriages, deaths), population registers, census records, military service, land and property records, tax lists and notary public records. Except for the Civil Registry, most of these records have not been filmed by the FHL and can only be studied in the archives of Belgium. The legal standing of the parish records was abrogated. [10]

Before we analyze the Civil Registry in detail, we add a few notes on some of the other civil records.

POPULATION REGISTERS- *Bevolkingsregisters*

As a complement to the civil registers, the population registers are the most important genealogical source. In 1796 French law required the municipalities to keep a "state of the population" in which all important information about a household would be recorded: the names, profession, birth dates, marriage, death, registration in the municipality, transfers to other towns, military service, etc. The early population registers were not always complete but on 3 September 1839 - during the Dutch period- a new law was promulgated which greatly improved the gathering of information. From 1 January 1847 the Belgian State made the population registers obligatory, and even today they are meticulously kept up by the municipalities. They were updated after each 10 year census.

These registers are preserved in the municipalities in Flanders and only one town's records have been filmed by the FHL: Antwerp 1800-1920 (no less than 600 microfilm rolls!)- so if you know in what municipality your ancestors resided, you might have to travel to Belgium to consult these documents. (N.B. Registers younger than a 100 years are usually not available to the researcher.)

CENSUS RECORDS - *Volkstelling*

As a precurser and a complemetary source of the population registers, we have the census records. During the French period there are census for the year III (1794) , year IV-V, VII and VIII. The Dutch produced one in 1814-1815. In 1829 the Dutch government decided to have a census every ten years and the practice was continued from then on. The records are kept in the capitals of the provinces and in the general state archives (*Rijksarchief*).

. If you are lucky, the municipality where your ancestors lived might be listed among the 216

---

[10] It should be noted that many parish records were maintained by the parish priests even after 1796. They continued to record the baptisms, marriages and deaths in their parish, but those were no longer part of the "official" records. To access these records, - which is not easy- you must rely on the diocesan and individual parish archives. Since they have godparents and family witnesses, they can be of great value.

microfilms on "census records Belgium" at the FHL.[11] If not, many of the census records of individual municipalties have been transcribed and published by local chapters of the VVF.

MILITARY RECORDS- *Militielijsten*

In 1789 the French introduced obligatory military service for men 2--25 years of age. The conscription lists can be found in the provincial repositories of the general State Archives (*Algemeen Rijksarchief*). These lists provide vital records on indiviuals, including their physical attributes.

CIVIL REGISTRY - *Burgerlijke stand*

All births, weddings and deaths were recorded in the Civil Registry (*Burgerlijke Stand*) of the municipalities. These documents, redacted in French (until 1815 and often beyond) or Flemish (after 1815), were made in duplicate of which one copy remained in the archives of the municipality and the other was sent to the Court of First Instance (*Rechtbank van Eerste Aanleg*).

All Burgerlijke Stand records of the Flemish provinces up to ca 1900 have been microfilmed by the Family History Library and are easily accessible. [12] To find these records, go to the FHL website and click on their "Library Catalogue." From there go to *place search*, and fill in the town you are looking for. The town will, as a rule, have *church records,* and *civil records*. Click, civil records and the list will be displayed. Always click *film notes* in order to get an overview of the available films.

For records after 1900, one must go to the Civil Registry of the municipality itself. Although these records are "public", and you can obtain copies, the registrars are not obliged to let you research the records in person. You may obtain permission from the mayor - as I did in my hometown of Torhout- where a permission had to be discussed by the mayor and his aldermen...

Before you access the orginal document, it is advisable to consult the INDEXES (*klappers*) of the civil registry. In the French period 1796-1802 no indexes were officially made, although they were often added at a later time. **10-year indexes** starting with 1803-1812 are available on separate microfilms at the FHL. From the year 1807 the civil registrar was required to end the year with an **yearly index**. This alphabetical list is divided in several columns where you will find the names, numbers of the acts and dates. In the birth record, the name of the mother is listed. The marriage index lists both husband and wife alphabetically. In the death index, the widow or widower is often listed.

Remember!
- ☛ Watch for the spelling of the surnames: I have found *Goethals, Ghoetals, Goetals, Goethaels,* all belonging to the same family. The same can be said about other indexes such as the parish records.
- ☛ It is advisable to search for the surnames of in-laws in the index: the record might confirm

---

[11] Go to FHL library catalogue, click *keywords* and type *census records Belgium*.
[12] The FHL is in the process of filming civil registry records up to 1920.

or even reveal family links.

- Always make a photo copy of a document with data of interest: it avoids copying errors and you can always go back to the document later. Record the number of the FHL microfilm.
- Indexes are often found at the beginning or end of the orginal records. So always roll through the entire film first before you waste time in your search of original documents.
- Marriage records provide a multitude of information. It is advisable to start with the marriage records and then to transfer to births and deaths.
- In the birth records and the death records the date of the act is drawn up is not always the date of birth or the date of the death.

NAMEN EN VOORNAMEN		DAG	BLADZIJDE
VAN DEN MAN OF VAN DE VROUW.	VAN DE MEDEGEHUWDE.	DER AKTE.	VAN HET REGISTER.

Sample of a civil register marriage index: husband's name, wife's name, date of the act and page reference

These civil record sources are of great value to the researcher: the birth certificates provide the names of the parents, their ages, professions and residence. Wedding acts not only give data on the marriage partners but also on their parents, and similar data can be found in the death certificates. All these acts required witnesses who were not always family members but could be acquaintances, neighbors, or even "professional" witnesses who witnessed for a small fee. From the parish records one could often reconstruct family links because the baptismal godparents and wedding witnesses were usually family members. This is not always the case here.

We will guide you through three complete records in both Flemish and French: a birth record, a marriage record and a death record. Since the documents were written according to a set formula, you should be able to analyze any civil record you find about your relatives.

VITAL RECORDS IN FLEMISH

A. BIRTH RECORD- *Geboorteakte*

In all documents, **the date** is introduced by *In den jare* or *ten jare* - in the year. The sequence is: year, day, month, hour. Since the civil registers run from 1796 to 1900, there are only two important century numbers: *zeventien honderd* (seventeen hundred) and *achtienhonderd* (eighteen hundred), followed by the cardinal numbers:

1- *een*	6- *zes*	11- *elf*	16- *zestien*	30- *dertig*	80- *tachtig*
2- *twee*	7- *zeven*	12- *twaalf*	17- *zeventien*	40- *veertig*	90- *negentig*
3- *drie*	8- *acht*	13- *dertien*	18- *achttien*	50- *vijftig*	100- *honderd*
4- *vier*	9- *negen*	14- *veertien*	19- *negentien*	60- *zestig*	
5- *vijf*	10- *tien*	15- *vijftien*	20- *twintig*	70- *zeventig*	

From number 21 on the figures are formed by units followed by the tens ("two and twenty" *tweeëntwintig*); 33 = *drieendertig*; 67 = *zevenenzestig*.

Then follows the day, introduced by *den* (on the), followed by an ordinal number:

1st - *eersten*	6th- *zesden*	11th- *elfden*	16th- *zestienden*
2nd- *tweeden*	7th- *zevenden*	12th- *twaalfden*	17th- *zeventienden*
3rd- *derden*	8th- *achtsten*	13th- *dertienden*	18th- *achtienden*
4th- *vierden*	9th- *negenden*	14th- *veertienden*	19th- *negentienden*
5th- *vijfden*	10th- *tiende*	15th- *vijftienden*	20th- *twintigsten*

Beyond twenty, just add the cardinal number in front: 22nd : *twee en twintigsten* , etc.
The months are easily recognizable: Januari, September, etc. March=*Maart;* May= *Mei.*
The hour of the report : *ten zeven ure* (at seven o'clock) *en half* (and half); *voormiddag* (A.M.); *namiddag* (P.M.); *noen* or *middag* (noon); *middernacht* (midnight).

As a starting point, we are using the complete birth record of Charles Godderis, who died in Detroit on 12 December 1933. (He deserves to be called the " father of the Flemish American Societies in Detroit.")

The record has three parts:

      1) introductory lines

      2) the main record

      3) the closing lines

1. Introductory lines[13]

These include a) the date and hour of registration; b) the registrar's name and title; c) the place of registration

" *In den Jaere Achtienhonderd vijf en vijftig, den achtienden April, ten vijf uren namiddag, zijn voor ons, Mansuetus Spillebout, Burgemeester en ambtenaar van den burgerlyken stand der stad Rousselare, provintie Westvlaenderen....* "[14]

(In the year eighteen hundred and fifty-five, on the eighteenth of April, at five in the afternoon, [have before us - N.B. the "have" is connected to the second part "appeared"] Mansuetus Spillebout, mayor and officer of the civil registry of the city of Rousselare, province of West-Flanders)

The registrar's name follows *is* (has) or *zijn* (have) *voor ons* (before us) e.g. Mansuetus Spillebout. Sometimes this introduction is placed after the place of registration. Then follows the title of the registrar *burgemeester* (mayor) or *ambtenaar van den burgerstand* or *officier* (officer of the civil registration). In the absence of the mayor, a *schepen* or *gedelegeerde ambtenaar* (alderman or delegated officer) would take his place.

Three places are always mentioned, not necessarily in the same order: *gemeente* (municipality), *arrondissement* (district) and *provincie* (province). If the municipality is at the same time the seat of the district, the latter is usually omitted.

2. Main record

Here we find the following sequences: a) the declarant; b) the child's gender, date and place of birth; c) the mother of the child; d) the name of the child.

a) "... *gecompareerd LEONARDUS GODDERIS, oud negen en dertig jaren, potbakker, geboren en wonende te Rousselare.*(appeared LEONARDUS GODDERIS, old thirty -nine years, potter, born and living in Rousselare,)

The declarant, usually the father, is introduced by the words *is (zijn) verschenen* or *is gecompareerd* (has - or have-appeared)[15] . Then follows his age, occupation, place of birth and present residence.

---

[13] Since the introductory lines of marriage and death records follow exactly the same pattern, this explanation will not be repeated in the sections dealing with them.

[14] The English translation is given between brackets. **After the translation has been given once for a particular phrase, it will not be repeated in subsequent document examples.** Only new terms will be translated. All Flemish is in italics.

Het jaar Duizend acht honderd twee en veertig, den twintigsten Mei, om elf uren 'smorgens, zijn vóór ons Charles Boutens, Schepen Ambtenaar van den burgerstand der stad Thourout, provincie West Vlaanderen, verschenen: Auguste Vanmaele, schoenmaker oud des en twintig jaren, geboren te Thourout, den Derden january achttien honderd ses en dertig, en alhier woonende, Meerderjarige zoon van Karel en van Rosalie Bonnart, werklieden te Thourout wonende, alhier tegenwoordig en toestemmend in dit huwelyk. En Marie-Louise Rooseboom, werkster oud drie en twintig jaren, geboren te Thourout den negenden november achttien honderd acht en dertig en er meer Meerderjarige Dochter van Jan overleden te Thourout, den achtsten february achttien honderd twee en vestig, en van Rosalie Blomme, werkster te Thourout wonende, alhier tegenwoordig en toestemmend in dit huwelyk, alles blykende uit de hierbevens gevoegde Stukken, welke verschynen, na ons verklaard te hebben, dat er tusschen hun geen huwelyks kontrakt is opgemaakt geworden, ons verzocht hebben van te willen overgaan tot de voltrekking van het huwelyk onder hun beremd, en waarop de afkondigingen gedaan zyn geweest, voor de voornaamste ingang deur van het Stadhuis alhier, te weten de eerste den elfden en de tweede den achttienden der loopende maand Mei t'elkens 'smiddags, gezien het artificaat vereischt by het artikel twee honderd drie niet van den achtsten january achttienhonderd zeventien waar uit blykt, dat Auguste Vanmaele, aan de wet op de nationale Militie heeft voldaan, geen tegenstreving aan dit huwelyk ons te kennen gegeven zynde, zigt staand aan hun verzoek, hebben wij na Dat alle de stukken hier bovengemeld hun door ons waren voorgelezen, als mede het zesde Kapittel van het burgerwetboek handelende van het huwelyk, gevraagd aan de aanstaande echtgenoten of zy malkaar begeren aan te nemen voor Man en vrouw, elk van hun afzonderlyk geantwoord hebbende Ja, wy verklaren in den naam van de wet, dat: Auguste Van maele en Marie-Louise Rooseboom, door het huwelyk zyn vereenigd, van al het welk wij dezen akt opgemaakt hebben in tegenwoordigheid van Polydor Vandhournout, oud vier en twintig jaren, Hena Dekitelaere oud twee en dertig jaren beide byzonder, Bruno Dedijne werkman oud vier en veertig jaren en Louis Fonteyne Metselaar oud vyf en vyftig jaren, allen noch Maag noch bloedverwantschap der echtgenoten, en alle wonende te Thourout, Na lezing de bruidegom de bruid en haar Moeder, hebben benevens de getuigen dezen akt met ons geteekend, benevens de getuigen, de ouders van den bruidegom hebben verklaard niet te kunnen teekenen by onkunde.

Marriage civil record of the author's great-grandparents August Vanmaele and Marie Louise Rooseboom

*b) "...den welken ons vertoond heeft een kind van het Mansgeslacht, (*who has shown us a child of the masculine gender) *geboren (born) den zestienden dezer maand* (of this month) *ten zeven uren s'morgens in het huis* (in his house) *N° 12 Sint Amandusstraat in stad, van hem vertoonder..."*

If it was a girl the text would read *"of the vrouwelijk geslacht* "(of the feminine gender).[16] Then follows the date of birth. That date is often replaced by *heden* (today), *gisteren* (yesterday), or *eergisteren* (the day before yesterday) and often the residence.

c) "...& van MARIA NOSEDA, oud een en veertig jaren, wynkelierster, zijne huisvrouwe, geboren en wonende (shop keeper, his house wife, born and living) *te Rousselare, ... "*

In case of an unwed mother we may find the expression *bevallen van een kind* (has delivered a child)....

d) "...& waer hy verklaerde te geven de voornaem van CAROLUS (where he declared to be given the first name of *CAROLUS.*) The name of the child was usually written in Latin.

3. Closing Lines

Here we find the names, ages, occupations and places of residence of two other witnesses, followed by their signatures. If they were illiterate, it was mentioned in this section.

" *Deze vertoning en verklaring gedaen in tegenwoordigheid van* (this presentation and declaration (was) done in the presence of) *Joseph Muylle, oud een en zestig jaren, pypmaker,* (pipefitter) *& van Petrus Sanctorum, oud een en veertig jaren, werkman, beide alhier wonende.*(laborer, both living here.) *Na voorlezing van deze akte de Vader en tweede getuige hebben met ons geteekend,* (After reading of this act the father and the second witness) *de eerste getuige verklarende niet te kunnen schryven by onkunde.* (the first witness declaring that he could not write)"

B. MARRIAGE RECORD- *Huwelijksakte*

As an example we will use the marriage record of Peter De Coster, born in 1830 and married in 1840, first consul of Belgium in Detroit. [17]

1. Introductory Lines

" *In het jaar achttien honderd veertig, den dertigsten september ten twee en half uren namiddag voor ons Romanus Vanden Hende, gemagtigde schepen by resolutie van vyftiende januari laest tot het opstellen der akten van den Burgerlijke Stand der Stad Aelst,*(alderman authorized by resolution of the 15th of January last, for the drawing of records of the civil registration of the town of Aalst...) *zijn gecompareerd..."*

For a translation we refer to the introductory lines of the birth records.

---

[16] It is notable that the declarant had to "show" the child to the registrar: the French had no doubt that they would stay for good in the Southern Netherlands and wanted to be sure they had a record of the gender of the new "citizens" so that later they could recruit him into the army. It seems that this gender identification rule still existed after Napoleon was defeated and that the terminology was kept in recording even after the rule was gone.

[17] *Flemish American Heritage,* Vol.I, N°1, p.14

2. Main Record

a/ Bridegroom and Bride

" *Petrus Decoster, meerderjarigen* (of age) *jongman* (single man) *agierende aldus over zich zelven,* (acting thus on his behalf) *oud dertig jaren, organist, geboren* (born) *te St. Lievens-Essche, provintie Oost Vlaenderen, woonachtig* (living in) *te Sint-Lievens-Essche, zone van* (son of) *Franciscus Decoster, geboortig* (born) *van St Lievens-Essche aldaer overleden* (there deceased), *en van wijlen* (late) *Francisca Temmerman, geboortig van St.Lievens-Esche, aldaer overleden, toekomende Bruydegom* (future bridegroom) *ter eenre* (on the one hand)... "

" *en Maria Elisabeth Torrini, meerderjarige jonge dochter* (single girl of age) *vergezeld door hare moeder toestemmende in dit huwelijk* (accompanied by her mother consenting to this marriage), *oud vyf en twintig jaren, naeyster* (seamstress) *geboren te Aelst, provintie Oost Vlaenderen, woonachtig te Aelst, dochter* (daughter) *van wijlen Stephanus Torrini, geboortig van San Martino Farnello, overleden te Aelst, en van Anna de Kempeneer, geboortig van Assche, woonachtig te Aelst, toekomende bruyd* (future bride) *ter andere* (on the other hand) "

b/ Witnesses

" *Welke vergezeld met door hun aengezochte en gekozen getuygen, te weten* ..(who accompanied by the witnesses invited and chosen by them, namely...) The names of the witnesses are followed by their ages, occupations and places of residence.

c/ Request and Publications

This part is an official request to perform the marriage and a record of the official publication and posting of the marriage in the municipalities of the marriage partners.

"...*ons verzogt hebben* (have requested us) *, over te gaan, tot het voltrekken van het huwelijk (*to proceed with the performing of their marriage), *waer van de afkondigingen en aanplakkingen zijn gedaen* (of which the publication and posting were done) *te Aelst en Sint Lieven-Essche den twintigsten en zeven en twintigsten dezer maand.* "

d/ Consent and Pronouncement

The marriage pronouncement begins with the words *Wy publiken ambtenaer van den Burgerlijke Stand, geen beletsel van oppositie opzigtelijk het tegenwoordig huwelyk hebbende...* " (We, public officer of the Civil Registration, not having any impediment or opposition regarding this present marriage...) and ends with *in huwelyk vereenigt zijn* (are united in marriage). The pronouncement was conditioned by the presentation of all the necessary documents (the dossier) before the registrar.

3. Supporting Documents (dossier) *Dossiers van Huwelijksbijlagen*

A series of supporting documents had to be presented before a marriage could be performed. These documents, produced by both parties, were kept in a dossier and deposited at the court together with the marriage record. These often overlooked dossiers can be a treasure for the researcher. Among its possible documents are :

- birth records of the marriage partners
- death records of the parents
- acts of divorce
- military service records
- acts of permission for the marriage
- proof of a pre-nuptial agreement
- proof of the publication and posting of the marriage plans, et. al.

A number of these dossiers have been placed on microfilm by the FHL and are listed under the municipalities next to the civil records. Dossiers less than a 100 years old can only be obtained by permission from a court. (Belgian Civil Law, article 45, § 1)

4. Closing Lines

" *van welk alles wy de tegenwoordige acte hebben opgemaakt* (from all of these -i.e. the supporting documents- we have drawn up the present act) *die na gedaene voorlezing is onderteekend in dubble door ons* (which after public reading is signed in duplicate by us), *de echtgenooten, de moeder der echtgenoote* (the spouses, the mother of the bride) *en de dry eertse getuygen* (and the first three witnesses) *den vierde getuygen heeft verklaard niet te konnen schryven* (the fourth witness has declared not being able to write)."

Postscript : **The Marriage Booklet** - *Het Trouwboekje*

The marriage booklet, officially introduced 14 November 1866, was the result of the cooperation between the civil and clerical powers in Belgium. Although more a custom than a legal requirement, it serves as a marriage certificate and contains important data on the marriage partners. Births and deaths are recorded, and often church marriages and baptisms are entered.

C. DEATH RECORD *Overlijdensakte*

The **introductory lines** of the death record are similar to the birth records: the date, name of the registrar and the place of registration. The **main record** names the witnesses who are reporting the death and includes information about the deceased. Here is an example of the latter:

"*Franciscus Vaneygen, oud zestig jaren, landbouwer (farmer), geboren te Cortemarck en wonende in deze gemeente* (living in this town), *zoon van Alexandeer Vaneygen en Isabella Vanghavers, landbouwers, beiden overleden* (both deceased) *te Cortemarck, echtgenoot van Maria Jacoba Pecceu, oud een en zestig jaren, wonende in deze gemeente, overleden is* (has died) *op gister* (yesterday) *negen en twintigsten dezer, ten elf ure's voormiddags,*(at 11 A.M.) *in zijn woonhuis binnen deze gemeente.*(in his home within this town)"

The record closes with the signatures of the witnesses.

The form of the death acts has remained quite constant through the years. The witnesses may be related to the deceased, be acqaintances or neighbors. If not related it is usually mentioned as *geen bloedverwant* (no blood relation), *gebuur* (neighbor) or *vriend* (friend).

Sample of a marriage booklet of 1926 in Aarsele:
Hector Lambrecht & Maria Clara Tavernier
(note that the church wedding is added)

ᵥ ᵥ ᵥ

The transcription of civil records in Flemish towns into the French language was the result of the invasion of the Southern or Autrian Netherlands by the French Revolutionary Armies in 1794. Official documents remained in French until Napoleon was defeated in 1814.

After the annexation to France, the French Republican Calendar was introduced in Flanders and the nine provinces were given new names. The basic format of the French civil records is identical to the Flemish ones described above. In this section we will provide you with the translations of the French terminology and other necessary data.

THE FRENCH REPUBLICAN CALENDAR

After the French Revolution in 1789, the "Convention" proclaimed the French Republic on 22 September 1792. By decree of 5 October 1793, a new " Republican Calendar" was to replace the old Gregorian Calendar, taking as the starting date 22 September 1792, which henceforth would be known as " 1 Vendemaire An 1 " (the first of Vendemaire of the Year 1). This decree was finalized 24 November 1793. The old Gregorian calendar was reintroduced on 23 December 1805.

The new calendar year was divided in 12 months of 30 days each, complemented by an additional month (*complémentaire*) of 5 days at the end of the year (or 6 days in a leap year). The names of the months were inspired by the seasons:

Fall	*Spring*
Vendémaire (wine-harvest)	Germinal (seed, shoot)
Brunaire (mist)	Floréal (flower, blossom)
Frimaire (frost)	Prairial (meadow)
Winter	*Summer*
Nivose (snow)	Messidor (harvest)
Pluviose (rain)	Thermidor (heat, bath)
Ventose (wind)	Fructidor (fruit)
	Complémentaire

Each year of the Republican Calendar begins around 22 September of the Old Calendar, and ends around 21 September of the next year: "An 1" begins on 1 Vendémaire (22 September 1792) and ends on 5 Complémentaire (21 September 1793).

"Translating" the Republican Calendar into the Gregorian one can be done with the help of 2 charts displayed on the next two pages. Suppose you want to translate the date "5 Nivose An 5" into that of the Gregorian Calendar.

⍦ When recording vital data from the French period, always give the Republican calendar date AND the "translated" date.

First you look in **Chart I** for "An 5"- it corresponds to 1796-1797, from around 22 September 1792 to around 21 September 1793. Next you look up the letter in the column under " An 5" that accords with Nivose, namely the letter "I".

THE FRENCH REPUBLICAN CALENDAR CHART I													
	an 1	an 2	an 3	an 4	an 5	an 6	an 7	an 8	an 9	an 10	an 11	an 12	an 13	an 14
years &months	1792	1793	1794	1795	1796	1797	1798	1799	1800	1801	1802	1803	1804	1805
	1793	1794	1795	1796	1797	1798	1799	1800	1801	1802	1803	1804	1805	
VENDEMAIRE Sept-Oct	P	P	P	R	P	P	P	R	R	R	R	T	R	R
BRUMAIRE Oct-Nov	K	K	K	O	K	K	K	O	O	O	O	S	O	O
FRIMAIRE Nov- Dec	J	J	J	P	J	J	J	P	P	P	P	R	P	P
NIVOSE Dec- Jan	I	I	I	K	I	I	I	K	K	K	K	O	K	K
PLUVIOSE Jan-Feb	G	G	G	I	G	G	G	I	I	I	I	K	I	##
VENTOSE Feb-Mar	M	M	M	L	M	M	M	N	N	N	N	O	N	##
GERMINAL Mar-Apr	I	I	I	I	I	I	I	K	K	K	K	K	K	##
FLOREAL Apr- May	H	H	H	H	H	H	H	J	J	J	J	J	J	##
PRAIRIAL May- Jun	G	G	G	G	G	G	G	I	I	I	I	I	I	##
MESSIDOR Jun- Jul	F	F	F	F	F	F	F	H	H	H	H	H	H	##
THERMIDOR Jul- Aug	E	E	E	E	E	E	E	G	G	G	G	G	G	##
FRUCTIDOR Aug- Sep	A	A	B	A	A	A	B	C	C	C	D	C	C	##

Now you go to **Chart II**. Look in the column under the letter "I"; the numbers run from 21 to 31 and then from 1 to 19. For Nivose, which is part of December and part of January, in year 5, the beginning date correpends to 21 December, the last day to 19 January. The numbers in the wide column at the left give the days of Nivose, 1 to 30. The fith day of Nivose lines up with the number 25 under the letter "I", or 25 December 1796.

THE FRENCH REPUBLICAN CALENDAR
CHART II

DAYS	A	B	C	D	E	F	G	H	I	J	K	L	M	N	O	P	Q	R	S	T
1 un	18	18	19	19	19	19	20	20	21	21	22	20	19	20	21	22	23	23	24	24
2 deux	19	19	20	20	20	20	21	21	22	22	23	21	20	21	22	23	24	24	25	25
3 trois	20	20	21	21	21	21	22	22	23	23	24	22	21	22	23	24	25	25	26	26
4 quatre	21	21	22	22	22	22	23	23	24	24	25	23	22	23	24	25	26	26	27	27
5 cinq	22	22	23	23	23	23	24	24	25	25	26	24	23	24	25	26	27	27	28	28
6 six	23	23	24	24	24	24	25	25	26	26	27	25	24	25	26	27	28	28	29	29
7 sept	24	24	25	25	25	25	26	26	27	27	28	26	25	26	27	28	29	29	30	**30**
8 huit	25	25	26	26	26	26	27	27	28	28	29	27	26	27	28	29	30	**30**	**31**	1
9 neuf	26	26	27	27	27	27	28	28	29	29	30	28	27	**28**	**29**	**30**	**31**	1	1	2
10 dix	27	27	28	28	28	28	29	29	30	**30**	**31**	**29**	**28**	1	1	1	1	2	2	3
11 onze	28	28	29	29	29	29	30	**30**	**31**	1	1	1	1	2	2	2	2	3	3	4
12 douze	29	29	30	30	30	**30**	**31**	1	1	2	2	2	2	3	3	3	3	4	4	5
13 treize	30	30	**31**	**31**	**31**	31	1	2	2	3	3	3	3	4	4	4	4	5	5	6
14 quatorze	**31**	**31**	1	1	1	1	2	3	3	4	4	4	4	5	5	5	5	6	6	7
15 quinze	1	1	2	2	2	2	3	4	4	5	5	5	5	6	6	6	6	7	7	8
16 seize	2	2	3	3	3	3	4	5	5	6	6	6	6	7	7	7	7	8	8	9
17 dix-sept	3	3	4	4	4	4	5	6	6	7	7	7	7	8	8	8	8	9	9	10
18 dix-huit	4	4	5	5	5	5	6	7	7	8	8	8	8	9	9	9	9	10	10	11
19 dix-neuf	5	5	6	6	6	6	7	8	8	9	9	9	9	10	10	10	10	11	11	12
20 vingt	6	6	7	7	7	7	8	9	9	10	10	10	10	11	11	11	11	12	12	13
21 vingt-et-un	7	7	8	8	8	8	9	10	10	11	11	11	11	12	13	12	12	13	13	14
22 vingt-deux	8	8	9	9	9	9	10	11	11	12	12	12	12	13	14	13	13	14	14	15
23 vingt-trois	9	9	10	10	10	10	11	12	12	13	13	13	13	14	15	14	14	15	15	16
24 vingt-quatre	10	10	11	11	11	11	12	13	13	14	14	14	14	15	16	15	15	16	16	17
25 vingt-cinq	11	11	12	12	12	12	13	14	14	15	15	15	15	16	17	16	16	17	17	18
26 vingt-six	12	12	13	13	13	13	14	15	15	16	16	16	16	17	18	17	17	18	18	19
27 vingt-sept	13	13	14	14	14	14	15	16	16	17	17	17	17	18	19	18	18	19	19	20
28 vingt-huit	14	14	15	15	15	15	16	17	17	18	18	18	18	19	20	19	19	20	20	21
29 vingt-neuf	15	15	16	16	16	16	17	18	18	19	19	19	19	20	21	20	20	21	21	22
30 trente	16	16	17	17	17	17	18	19	19	20	20	20	20	21	22	21	21	22	22	23

Complementary days
at the end of the year

	A	B	C	D	E
1		17	17	18	18
2		18	18	19	19
3		19	19	20	20
4		20	20	21	221
5		21	21	22	22
6		# #	22	# #	23

PROVINCES AND DEPARTMENTS

The names of provinces of the Southern Netherlands were changed into departments during the French occupation.

Anvers	Antwerpen	Département des Deux-Nèthes	Twee Neten
Brabant	Brabant	" de la Dyle	Dijle
Flandre Orientale	Oost Vlaanderen	" de l"Escaut	Schelde
Flandre Occidentale	West Vlaanderen	" de la Lys	Leie
Hainaut	Henegouwen	" de Jemmapes	Jemapes
Liège	Luik	" de l'Ourthe	Jemapes
Limbourg	Limburg	" de la Meuse-Inférieure[18]	Beneden-Maas
Luxembourg	Luxemburg	" des Forêts	Wouden
Namur	Namen	" de la Sambre-et-Meuse "	Samber-en-Maas

TOWNS

In the French civil records Flemish town names usually were translated into French: *Brugge* became *Bruges*, *Kortrijk* became *Courtrai*, *Antwerpen* became *Anvers,* etc. If you are trying to find records for a certain Flemish town in Belgian or FHL library catalogues, it is advisable to use the official Flemish spelling of the town - such as "Brugge, Antwerpen"- and the French spelling for towns in the French-speaking part of Belgium - such as "Liège, Namur." This also applies if you ever visit Flanders and are looking in vain for a road sign to "Louvain" (Leuven)!

FRENCH NUMBERS

The cardinal numbers are used for the date of the month from 2 to 30. For the first day of the month *"le premier "* (the first) is used.

2- *deux*	8- *huit*	14- *quatorze*	20- *vingt*	26- *vingt-six*
3- *trois*	9- *neuf*	15- *quinze*	21- *vingt-et-un*	27- *vingt-sept*
4- *quatre*	10- *dix*	16- *seize*	22- *vingt-deux*	28- *vingt-huit*
5- *cinq*	11- *onze*	17- *dix-sept*	23- *vingt-trois*	29- *vingt-neuf*
6- *six*	12- *douze*	18- *dix-huit*	24- *vingt-quatre*	30- *trente*
7- *sept*	13- *treize*	19- *dix-neuf*	25- *vingt-cinq*	

From 1795 to 1805 - the Republican Calendar- records begin with " *L'an* (year) ... *de la république..."*

---

[18] The Département de la Meuse-Inférieure included present day Belgian and Dutch Limburg, while the Département des Forêts included present day Belgian Luxemburg and the Grand Duchy of Luxemburg. These territories were still part of Belgium until 1839 when Dutch Limburg and the Grand Duchy of Luxemburg were separated and placed under the king of the Netherlands.

After 1805, cardinal numbers are used *mille huit cent cinq* (one thousand eight hundred and five) or *dix-huit cent cinq* (eighteen hundred and five)

40--*quarante* 50- *cinquante*   60- *soixante*   100- *cent*

Be careful with the following numbers:

70- soixante-dix (sixty and ten) e.g. soixante cinq (65); soixante dix-sept (76)
                 Sometimes you'll find the Belgian French term *septante*.
80- quatre-vingt (four x twenty) e.g. quatre-vingt-huit (88)
90- quatre-vingt-dix (four x twenty + ten) e.g. quatre-vingt-onze (91) or the Belgian French term
                                           nonante.

The time is expressed in *heures* (hour), followed by *matin* (morning)*; midi* (noon) *après-midi* (afternoon)*; soir* (evening) *nuit* (night) *and minuit* (midnight).

A. BIRTH RECORD - *Acte de Naissance*

As a model, we use the birth record of Father Peter Francis Beauprez, a Flemish missionary who came to the U.S.A. as a seminarian in 1828. He worked in the dioceses of Arkansas, New Orleans, and Milwaukee, where he died in 1846.

1. Introductory lines

" *L'An treize de la république le vingt du mois Nivose* (of the month Nivose) *à neuf heures du matin* (at nine in the morning), *pardevant nous maire de la Commune* (before us mayor of the town) *de Woumen, arrondissement de Furnes* (Veurne) *département de la Lys...* "

2. Main record

"... *est comparu* (has appeared) *François Beauprez tonnelier* (cooper) *demeurant et natif de Woumen* (resident and native of) *agé de soixante ans* (61 years old) *lequel nous a présenté* (who has presented to us) *un enfant de sexe masculin* (a child of the masculin gender) *né hier à cinq heures après midi* (born yesterday at five in the afternoon) *de lui déclarant* (from him the declarant) *et de Régine Rosalie Vansteene natif à Saint Jacobs Chapelle agé de trente neuf ans son épouse,* (his wife) *et auquel il a déclaré* (to whom he declared) *voiloir donner les prénoms* (to want to give the first names) *de Pierre François.*

3. Closing Lines

"*Les dites déclaration et présentation faites en présence* (the said declaration and presentation made in the presence of) *de Louis Blomme, Clerc* (clerk) *à Woumen et de F. Blomme écrivain* (writer) *à Woumen et ont signé avec nous le présent acte de naissance après qu'il leur en a été fait lecture* (and have signed with us the present act of birth after reading hereof was made to them)."

B. MARRIAGE RECORD - *Acte de Mariage*

1. Introductory Lines

"L'An mil huit cent onze le quatre février à quatre heures de relevée, pardevant nous Pierre Albert Denecker maire, <u>officier de l'état civil</u> (officer of the civil registry) *de la commune de Passchendaele troisième arrondissement du département de la Lys..."*

2. Main Record

a/ The Bridegroom and Bride

"...<u>sont comparus</u> (have appeared) *Jean Baptiste Lefebre agé de trente un ans <u>quatre mois cinq jours</u>* (4 months 5 days) <u>*né et cultivateur*</u> (born and farmer) *demeurant dans cette commune <u>fils majeur</u>* (major son) <u>*de feu*</u> (the late) *Bonaventure et de feue Pétronille Pattyn décédé(s) à Moorslede le quatre frimaire an douze et le vingt-huit Décembre dix-sept cent quatre-vingt-seize <u>comme il est constaté par l'acte de décès délivré au dit</u>* (as is stated in the death record delivered in said) *Moorslede le quatre février dix huit cent douze et de Jacqueline Descamps agée de vingt-sept ans neuf mois huit jours née et fille de cultivateur demeurante à Moorslede <u>fille majeure</u>* (major daughter) *de Guillaume <u>ci présent et consentant</u>* (here present and consenting) *et de feue Marie Thérèse Verdoolaege décédée à Moorsledele dix-sept septembre dix-sept cent quatre-vingt-dix sept..."*

b/ The Request and Publication of Marriage

"...<u>lesquels nous ont requis de procéder à la célébration de mariage projeté entre eux</u> (who have requested us to proceed with the marriage planned between them) *et <u>dont les publications ont été faites devant la principale porte de notre maison commune</u>* (and whose publications have been made before the main door of our town hall) *savoir la première le dix-neuf janvier dix-huit cent douze à l'heure du midi et la seconde le vingt-six du même mois à l'heure du midi..."*

c/ The Documents, Consent and Pronouncement

"... <u>aucune opposition au dit mariage ne nous ayant été signifiée</u> (no opposition to this marriage having been made to us) <u>*faisant droit à leur requisition*</u> (complying to their request), <u>*après avoir donné lecture de toutes les pièces ci-dessus mentionnées*</u> (after having given reading of all the documents heretofore mentioned) *et <u>du chapître six du code napoléon intitulé mariage</u>* (and of the sixth chapter of the Code of Napoleon entitled 'about marriage') <u>*avons demandé au futur époux et à la future épouse s'ils veulent se prendre pour marie et pour femme*</u> (have asked the future husband and the future wife if they want to take each other for husband and wife) <u>*chacun d'eux ayant répondu séparément et affirmativement*</u> (each of them having responded separately and affirmatively), <u>*déclarons au nom de la loi*</u> *que Jean Baptiste Lefevre et ladite Jacoba Descamps <u>sont unis par le mariage</u>* (declare in the name of the law that Jean Baptiste Lefebre and the said Jacoba Descamps are united in marriage.)

d/ The Witnesses

" <u>de quoi nous avons dressé acte en présence de</u> ..." (whereof we have drafted the record in presence of) The names, age, occupation, and possible family relation is mentioned here.

3. Closing Lines

" *Lesquels après qu'il leur a été faite lecture,* (who after reading of it) *ont signé avec nous et les partis contractants* (have signed with us and the contracting parties) *excepté* le dit Guillaume et Joseph Descamps, *père et frère de la future épouse qui ont déclaré de ne savoir écrire après lecture faite.* (except...father and brother of the future wife, who have declared not to be able to write, after the reading was made)

C. DEATH RECORDS

The death records should not present a translation problem. The format is similar to the Flemish record above, and the French terminology is already present in the birth and marriage records.

First page of the parish records
of St Jacob Church in Gent

"Baptismal register
in which are kept the names
of the baptized in said
parish; also the names
of the godparents with precise
annotation of the day
of the baptism. Added is
also, by order
of the bishop, the day and hour
of the birth of the child, under
the signature of the pastor or
his substitute. Beginning
from the year one thousand six
hundred and forty six

To the greater
glory of God"

III. THE PARISH RECORDS

It was not until after the Council of Trent (15 December 1545 - 12 April 1563) that parish priests in Europe were required to keep records of all baptisms and marriages. In the Southern Netherlands, this recording became obligatory in 1564 but was still very irregularly applied. In article 20 of their "Eternal Edict", on 12 July 1611, the rulers of Flanders, Albert and Isabella ordered the aldermen of towns and villages throughout their reign to make copies of all church records. Unfortunately, not many towns followed the edict. A century and a half later, on March 6 1754, Maria Theresia issued an ordinance requiring new copies of all church records up to that time. Thus the parish registers were preserved as two separate sources: church and magistracy. Except for some very early records, all were written in Latin. On 17 June 1796 (29 Prairial IV) the French introduced the civil registration system, thereby officially ending the parish registers.

The parish records are invaluable sources to the researcher: they give the date of baptism and birth, and the names of both parents and godparents. Grandparents were customarily chosen as godparents of the first child; in most cases siblings were chosen as sponsors. Often the records reveal other data, such as the profession of the father and the parish of origin of the parents. They even indicate the social status of the family, as when "important" people in town were chosen to be godparents or when they were buried inside the church.

Almost all parish records are in Latin. Since the parish priests followed a set formula for each record, it is not that difficult to decipher a record after studying the examples analyzed and translated below.

The Indexes - *Klappers*

The Belgian government decided in 1863 to have indexes made of all existing parish registers in the country. Just as was done with the civil records, one copy was to be deposited in the archives of the municipality, and the other was sent to the Court of First Instance (*Rechtbank van Eerste Aanleg*). The indexes, or *klappers* in Flemish, cover baptisms, weddings and burials. The alphabetical lists provide the names of the baptized children, often the names of the parents, the date of baptism and the page number of the original document. For the marriage records, the marriage partners are listed individually. In the death records, the name of the wife (or widow) or husband (or widower) are often added - a sure way to identify them.

The enormous work of indexing all these records was left to municipal employees who were paid by the state per copy: as a result, more effort was often given to quantity than to quality! Although the indexes are certainly the first place you should look when researching the parish records, there are many pitfalls.

It is almost impossible to create your family tree by relying exclusively on the indexes: collect the information from the indexes, but always analyze the original parish registers. The indexers were not necessarily trained in reading old script and skipped names and entire records when they had a problem deciphering them: there are many N.N.s (nomen nescio- I don't know the name) in the records. At times, you will find family records in the registers which were not recorded in the indexes.

There are gaps in the indexes because of the loss of the original records and/or their copies due to the religious wars and the two world wars.

We suggest you also make a record of the in-laws, which may help you later in reconstructing the family.

Practically all the indexes and the original parish records of the Belgian provinces have been filmed by the FHL and are available in the US. To find them, go to the Family History Website (< familysearch.org >) - Library Catalogue and click *place search;* enter your parish; click *church records;* click *vieuw filmnotes.* The indexes and the original records are listed here. Click on *print version* and print out the list. We suggest strongly that you print the list as a future source reference and an easy way to order the films.

Page of a parish marriage index.(klapper)
(St. Amandus Church, Ingelmunster)

The Parish Registers- *De Parochieregisters*

The endless hours of examining the parish records have taught us some important lessons. The following suggestions may prevent you from wasting your time and " If I only had..." moments!

- As a rule, look through the entire film at the beginning of your search: you may find that there are unexpected indexes; there may be gaps in the record: for example,the records "1735-1795" only cover "1735-1740 and 1780-1796"; there may be two separate versions of the record: the hard-to-read originals and the easy-to-read copies made at a later time.
- The death records are usually short and do not give more than the name of the deceased and the date of his death. To identify the deceased further, "husband, widower, wife, widow" will be mentioned. Take with a grain of salt the age given at death: give or take 5 years - birth certificates were not issued at that time.
- If you are in luck, the indexers have written names in the margin of the originals: an easy tool if you peruse the entire record. Check also the documents of in-laws.
- In early records, the name of the mother is often missing, or only the christian name is given. The same happens to godmothers as they give the christian name and "wife of ..."
- The burials of small children are often not recorded although they were sometimes listed in a separate record. When you find two children with an identical name, it does not necessarily mean that the first child died: from other sources we learn that sometimes they gave the same name to more than one child.
- Before you return your film, go through the entire record once more to make sure you did not miss anything and you may not have to pay a new fee later on!
- Make copies of individual records for later use. You may find out later that parts of the text you could not understand or read later became obvious! And of course, always take note of the film number and page where you found your source.
- When ordering parish records, it may be wise to order some of neighboring parishes because people usually lived in a very limited area.
- Make a copy of the individual record AND a copy of the entire page. This may assist you in deciphering the penmanship of the writer.
- Sometimes the recorder only wrote down the date for the individual act: you may have to consult the previous pages to find the month and the year.

A. BAPTISM RECORD - *Doopact*

In its skeletal format, a baptism record always contains the following elements: 1. the time of baptism and birth; 2. the name and gender of the child; 3. the parents; 4. the godparents.

In records of the 18th century other elements were added: e.g. the ages of the parents, their profession, their parish of origin, etc. [19]

The **time** of baptism includes: year, month, day and hour.

The **year** is usually written in numbers at the beginning of a new year, or repeated at the top of the page, or in each entry. It may be proceeded by *anno (domini)* .

The **month** is written at the beginning of a month section or repeated in each entry usually in the nominative case: *Januarius* If preceeded by *in* the ablative case is used and the month is still easily recognizable.

Januarius	*Aprilis*	*Julius*	*October (8ber - VIIIber)*
Februarius	*Maius*	*Augustus*	*November (9ber- IXber)*
Martius	*Junius*	*September (7ber- VIIber)*	*December (10ber- Xber)*

Each entry begins with the word *die* (on the ... **day**) written in numbers or in full - e.g. *die 1* or *die prima.*

1 ª	*prima*	*7 ª*	*septima*	*13 ª*	*decima tertia*	*19 ª*	*decima nona*
2 ª	*secunda*	*8 ª*	*octava*	*14 ª*	*decima quarta*	*20 ª*	*vigesima*
3 ª	*tertia*	*9 ª*	*nona*	*15 ª*	*decima quinta*	*21 ª*	*vigesima prima*
4 ª	*quarta*	*10 ª*	*decima*	*16 ª*	*decima sexta*	*30 ª*	*trigesima*
5 ª	*quinta*	*11 ª*	*undecima*	*17 ª*	*decima septima*	*31 ª*	*trigesima prima*
6 ª	*sexta*	*12 ª*	*duodecima*	*18 ª*	*decima octava*	*die ultima* (last day)	

At times the numerical date is replaced by other expressions: *hodie* (today); *eadem die* (the same day); *heri* or *pridie* (yesterday); *nudius tertius* (the day before yesterday); *die ultima precedentis mensis* (last day of last month).

The hour is introduced by *hora* (at the hour): *ante meridiem* (A.M.), or *mane, matutina; post meridiem* or *vesperi* or *vespertina* (P.M.); *meridie* (12 noon); *media nocte* (midnight); *noctis* (of the night); *et dimidia* (half hour); *circa , ca.* (approximately).

Lets look at an example: "*baptizatus est Joannes, filius (f ᵘˢ) legitimus Petri Goethals et Maria Tavernier, conjugum*...(is baptized Joannes legitimate son of Petrus Goethals and Maria Tavernier, spouses) or " *ego baptizavi Joannem filium Petri Goethals et Maria Tavernier, conjugum...*" (I have baptized ...)

For a girl the gender changes to *filia f ª legitima.* After *baptizatus est* the endings will be the nominative case *-us, -a* ; after *baptizavi*, the endings will be *-um, -am, -em* in the accusative case.[20]

---

[19] The *ex* (from) does not always indicate the parish where they were baptized, it may just point to where they lived or worked.

[20] In Latin, most masculine names end in -us and feminine names in -a. There are exceptions: Matthias, Sylvester, Agnes, Mechtildis, etc.

Notice that the mother is mentioned by her maiden name. Notice also the term *legitimus*, and *conjugum* (=lawfully married). For illegitimate children you can find the expressions *illegitimus, spurius(-a), extra matrimomium* (out of wedlock) or *pater ignotus* (father unknown).

- ❧ The first names are often in a different case: the genitive (Petri, Mariae, Felicitatis) , accusative (Petrum, Mariam, Feliciatem) or ablative (Petro, Maria, Felicitate). When recording it is advisable to use the first name in the nominative case: Petrus, Maria, Felicitas.
- ❧ The date of the baptism is not always the date of birth. Further in the text, you might find the expressions *natus eadem die* (born the same day) or *heri* (yesterday) or *postridie* (the day before yesterday).

The **godparents** follow the expression *susceperunt (suscepere* - abbreviated *susc.)* or *susceptores* (literally "the holders"). Sometimes the term *patrini* is used.

As noted above, sometimes the place of origin of the parents or sponsors is added: *ex* (from); *ex hac* (from this parish) or *incolarum hujus, hujus, hic habitans* (living here).

Finally there is some terminology that indicates special circumstances: baptized under condition - *sub conditione;* baptized by a midwife - *ab obstetrice;* in danger of death - *in periculo mortis, in articulo mortis;* a convert from Protestantism - *conversus (conversa) ex Protestantismo- conversus ex heresi* .

It is not difficult to notice baptisms of the offspring of V.I.P.s (members of the council, bayliffs, lawyers, canons, well-to-do burghers, etc): the baptism was usually perfomed by the parish priest himself and not by an assistant priest; the writing often became a little larger than the rest of the page and was more readable; and special adjectives were added to the parents and godparents: *nobilissimus, illustrissimus, reverendissimus, dominus, domicilla...*

B. MARRIAGE RECORD - *Huwelijksact*

The marriage ceremony was performed in the parish of one of the spouses, as a rule in the parish of the bride.The *sponsalia* (engagement or bethrotal) often preceded the actual marriage. There may be two separate entries at the respective dates, or the entry of the marriage may be added on to the entry of the bethrotal. The entries may have the same witnesses or different ones.

The marriage record has always the following elements: 1/ date (see above); 2/ the bridegroom and bride; 3/ the witnesses 4/ the banns of marriage; 5/ special circumstances: e.g. dispensations from impediments and banns.

After the date, the following expressions are used: *contraxerunt* (they contracted) or *inierunt* (they were entered into) followed by *sponsalia* or *matrimonium* (abbr. matr.). Also : *matrimonium iuncti sunt* (they united in matrimony).

The names of the spouses may be followed by their place of birth or residence, and their age: *natus hic* (born here); *ex* (from); *hujus* (from this place). If it is a second marriage, you may find _viduus (v<u>us</u>)_ (widower) _vidua - v <u>a</u>_ (widow) followed by the name of the first spouse.

Church law required that the **banns of marriage** be announced three times. This is usually mentioned in the entry: _factis trium bannorum proclamationibus_ (the proclamation of the three banns having been made) or _praeviis tribus bannis_ (the three banns having preceded). Often special dispensation of the banns was given : _dispensatione trium bannorum obtenta_ (having obtained dispensation of the three banns) ; or _cum dispensatione bannorum...cum dispensatione in bannorum proclamationibus._

Other **dispensations** were needed from impediments to the marriage. When a Catholic married a non-catholic a dispensation from the impediment of "mixed religion" was to be obtained: _cum dispensatione in impedimento mixtae religionis;_ or from the impediment of "disparity of cult" , i.e. if the non-catholic is not baptized: _...in impedimento disparitatis cultus._

Dispensations from impediments of consanguinity (blood relationship) or affinity were needed for a legal marriage. Here are examples:

cum dispensatione ab impedimento consanguinitatis in secundo gradu collaterali (with dispensation from the impediment of consanguinity in the second collateral degree) i.e. between two first cousins; _in tertio gradu_ (third degree) i.e. beween two second cousins.

cum dispensation...affinitatis in primo gradu (affinity in the first degree), i.e. when a widower marries the sister of his deceased wife.

The **witnesses** were the priest and two or three other persons. In many cases these witnesses were the parents or siblings of the spouses- again an important element for household reconstruction or confirmation. An "important" family would often invite a V.I.P. to witness the marriage.

Witnesses are introduced by _coram me- infrascripto- et testibus_ (before me- the undersigned- and the witnesses) or _testes fuerunt_ (the witnesses were). If the witnesses of the bethrotal and the marriage were the same, the expression was _testibus iisdem._ The age and residence of the witnesses may be added.

C. DEATH RECORD - _Overlijdensact_

Initially the burials records were not required by the Council of Trent, although the parish priests often kept a personal record of the burials. Soon, however, they became a part of the parish records. These burial records are often very skeletal: they don't give more than the names of the deceased and the date of the burial. In time, more and more data were added: the date of death, the deceased's relationships, the kind and place of burial, the cause of death, etc. The list below analyses the Latin vocabulary of possible data encountered in a burial record.

1. Some entries give both dates of death and of burial: _obiit ... et sepultus (-a) est_ (died...and was buried); _sepelivi_ (I buried).
2. The age of the deceased may be given, but is not always accurate: _aetatis_

...*annorum...mensium   dierum...*(age...years...months...days);   for   infants:...*horarum* (hours)...*hebdomadarum* (weeks) or *recens natus* (recently born); for young people: *puellus...puella* (young boy...young girl); for an old person: *senex... octogenarius* (in his eighties).

3. Relationship: *vir* or *maritus* or *coniunx* (husband); *uxor* or *coniunx* (wife); *viduus, vidua* (widower, widow); children: *infans* (infant), *proles, filius* (son), *filia* (daughter), *frater* (brother), *soror* (sister); unmarried: *innuptus(-a), caelebs.*

4. Last sacraments: *post susceptionem Sacramentorum* (after having received the -last-sacraments). *(pre)munitus omnibus Sacramentis Matris Eeclesiae* (fortified by all the -last-sacraments of Mother Church). This was sometimes abbreviated to *ob.Ss:M:E.* If the age of the person is not given, the fact that the last sacraments were given indicates that the person was "of age', i.e. at least seven years of age.

5. The place of burial : *in cemeterio* (in the cemetery), sometimes followed by more detail *versus orientem* (to the east) for example. To be buried *in ecclesia* (in the church) or *in choro* was a sign of prominence or wealth.

6. The social standing and the prosperity of the family are reflected in the kind of funeral service they requested for their loved-ones. There were funerals of 1st, 2nd or 3rd class - *primae, secundae, tertiae classis.*

   First class funerals consisted of Scripture Services (the singing of nine lessons of the Divine office) and a Mass. The Latin names indicating first class funerals are: *cum officio solemni* (with a solemn office); *cum officio novum lectionum* (with an office of nine lessons); *cum sacro solemni* or *Missa solemni* (with a solemn Mass); *cum exequiis primae classis* (with a funeral of first class); *cum exequiis summis* (with the highest funeral). With this service, some extras were added: more candles, tolling of the church bells, and the number of officiating clergy. Persons of nobility usually provided for the distribution of bread to the poor at their funeral.

   In the second class funerals there were only six lessons and a Mass. They are indicated by *cum officio medio, cum officio sex lectionum, cum exequiis duplicibus, cum exequiis majoribus, cum exequiis mediis.*

   The third class was reduced to three lessons, and are indicated in Latin by *cum officio simplici, cum officio trium lectionum, cum exequiis simplicibus.* The following expressions would indicate a lesser funeral for a child or a poor person: *cum parvis exequiis* (with a small funeral); *ex charitate* (out of charity); *pauper* (a poor person).

7. Special circumstances. In times of war or plague services were delayed: *officium dilatum est* (the service was delayed); *peste* (from the plague); *ob bellum* (because of the war).

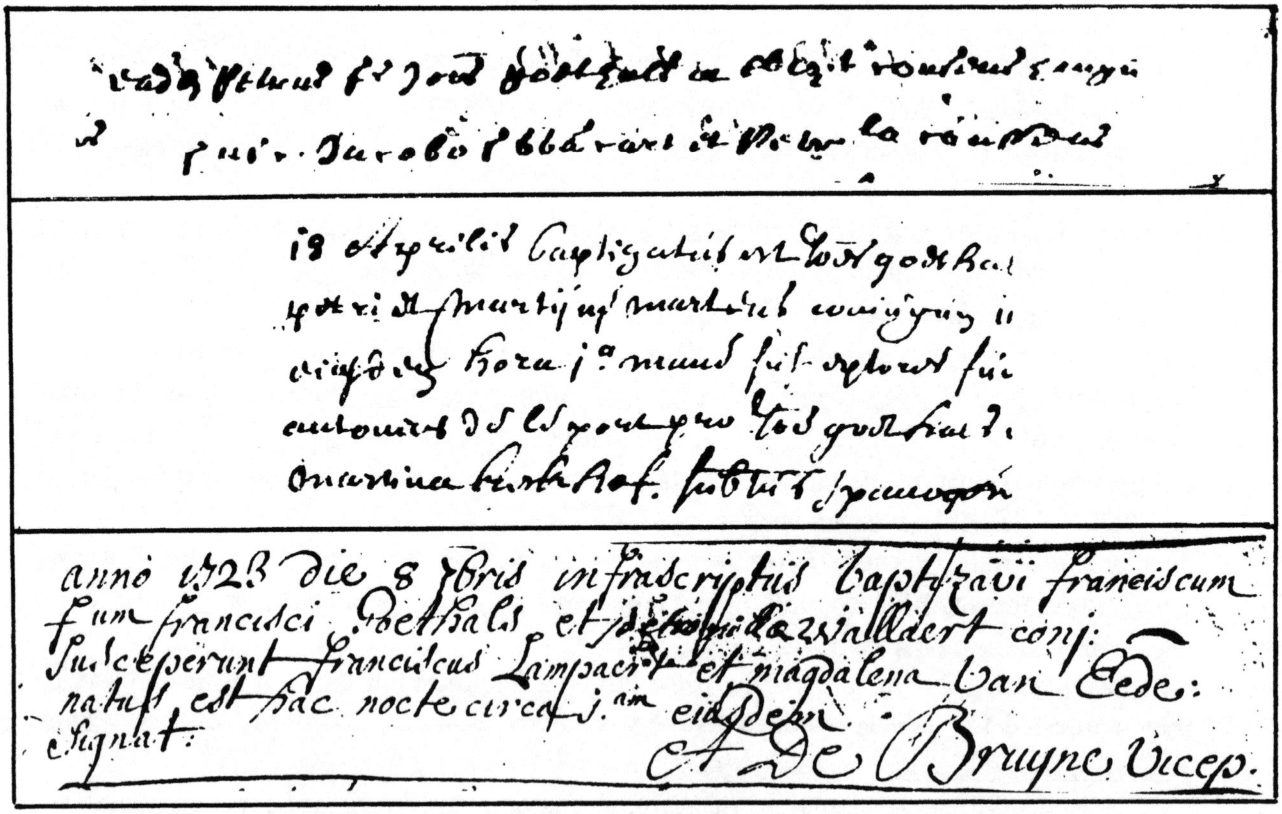

(Three handwritten baptism record samples, largely illegible cursive script)

anno 1723 die 8 7bris infrascriptus Baptizavi franciscum
fum francisci Goethals et ... Walraert conj:
Susceperunt franciscus Lampaert et magdalena van Eede.
natus est hac nocte circa i.am eiusdem
signat:
A De Bruyne Vicep.

Samples of baptism records, respectively of 1628, 1675 and 1723, illustrating the different scripts used by the parish priests or scribes.

vigesima Secunda maii 1776 factis tribus —
proclamationibus Coram me legitime matrimonio
juncti sunt petrus josephus goethals fs
petrijos. et barbara – teresia melier ex tieghem
nostri ... bus petro-josepho melier et pietro –
jos. goethals parentibus Sponsi et Sponsæ
... Steesen pastorin Emelghem

Marriage record of Josephus Goethals & Barbara Teresia Melier
Emelgem 22 May 177

Over the years I have developed an analysis method of parish records, which has served me well in identifying and/or confirming individuals as family members nd members of a household. For what it's worth, I want to share this method with the readers. You may adopt it literarily or modify it according to your own needs and preferences.

By carefully collecting all the possible information in a family sheet or "household record" one can come to reasoned conclusions about the identity of certain individuals.

The first thing to do is to collect *all the possible information* contained in a record. Record all this information in a household file. Below are two fictional generational households as a working example. Suppose you have collected the information on these two households : you suspect they are related but you are not sure!

(We are using the following abbreviations: b.= born; d.= death; m.= married; w.=witnesses; GP = godparents; // indicates the separation between information of two individuals)

Family A : Augustus Goethals & Maria Rosen

b, 23 Mar 1685 Pittem; d. 7 Jan 1743 Tielt // b. 18 Jul 1687 Torhout; d. 20 Dec 1752,
Tielt; fa Petrus Rosen.
m. 23 Jan 1712, Tielt; w. Josephus Goethals & Petrus Storme
children:
1. Petrus, 24 May 1713; GP Josephus Goethals & Rita Baeke
2. Maria, 6 Aug 1714, GP Theophilus Rosen & *Anna Goethals*
3. Josephus, 12 Nov 1716; d. 24 Dec 1718; GP *Arnoldus Goethals* & Jacobus Storme
4. Albertus, 8 Mar 1718; GP *Rogerius Goethals* & N.N. (not readable)
5. Petronella, 12 Feb 1720; GP Josephus Storme & *Joanna Goethals*

From the Family A household information we can infer data which might lead to the parents and siblings of Augustus Goethals born in Pittem in the 1685:

- the father of the groom (or a brother) was customarily a witness at the wedding: Josephus Goethals could be the father of Augustus- this could be confirmed later.

- brothers and sisters and in-laws were often godparents to a sibling's children: Augustus, therefore, could have had brothers *Arnoldus* and *Rogerius* and sisters *Joanna* and *Anna.*

Family B: Petrus Goethals & Annabella Pieters

b. 24 May 1713, Tielt; d. 18 Jan 1771, Tielt // b. 16 Apr 1718, Pittem ; fa Albertus &
Rosalia Opsomer
m. 10 Aug 1740, Tielt; w. Augustus Goethals & Albertus Pieters
1. Petrus Josephus, 10 Sep 1741; GP *Augustus Goethals* & Rosalia Opsomers
2. Jacobus, 2 Nov 1742; GP .. & *Petronella Goethals*
3. Rosalia, 8 Dec 1743;GP *Albertus Goethals* & Maria Tavernier

4. Regina, 12 May 1745; GP <u>Ludovicus Devriese</u> & *Maria Goethals*

5. Franciscus, 18 Sep 1746; GP <u>Paulus Bolle</u> & *Petronella Goethals*

Is this Petrus Goethals in Family B the son of Augustus in Family A?

We already know he was born 24 May 1713 in Tielt. Is he the same Petrus from family A?

- If no other baptism of a Petrus Goethals is found on that date in Tielt, then he is the one
- the witness at his wedding is Augustus
- Petronella, Maria, and Albertus , listed as brother and sisters in family A, are godparents of his children
- further research in Tielt revealed that a Maria Goethals was married to a Ludovicus Devriese in 1737, Paulus Bolle was married to a Petronella Goethals in 1743 , and an Albertus Goethals was married to Maria Tavernier in 1739. *Maria Tavernier, Ludovicus Devriese and Paulus Bolle are among the godparents of Petrus' children.*

This information gives us enough data to reasonably conclude that Petrus is indeed the son of Augustus and Maria Rosen. Now we can update the Augustus Goethals family A file by adding the marriage partners to his children (family A) "fs Augustus and Maria Rosen" to family B. We can repeat the same process when we come to the children of family B, etc.

Family A : Augustus Goethals & Maria Rosen (fs Josephus??)
b, 23 Mar 1685 Pittem; d. 7 Jan 1743 Tielt // b. 18 Jul 1687 Torhout;d. 20 Dec 1752,
Tielt; fa Petrus.
m. 23 Jan 1712, Tielt; w. Josephus Goethals & Petrus Storme

(married to)
1. Petrus, 24 May 1713; GP Josephus Goethals & Rita Baeke---------------Annabella Pieters 1740
2. Maria, 6 Aug 1714, GP Theophilus Rosen & *Anna Goethals*----------- Ludovicus Devriese 1737
3. Josephus, 12 Nov 1716; d. 24 Dec 1718; GP *Arnoldus Goethals* & Jacobus Storme
4. Albertus, 8 Mar 1718; GP *Rogerius Goethals* & N.N. ----------------------Maria Tavernier 1739
5. Petronella, 12 Feb 1720; GP Josephus Storme & *Joanna Goethals* -------------Paulus Bolle (1743)

The marriage partners are added to the children with the year of their wedding (or the year of their first child placed between brackets). Full information on their wedding and children will be added later in the chronological list.

Family B: Petrus Goethals & Annabella Pieters (fs Augustinus & Maria Rosen)

IV. OTHER SOURCES OF THE OLD REGIME

Besides the parish registers, there is an array of other valuable sources: the results of changing administrative institutions that faithfully recorded all the activities of the population they administered. For several reasons, a number of these sources are not easily available to the researcher in the U.S.A.

1. Not all these sources were recorded on microfilm by the Family History Library
2. Even if the originals were filmed, your knowledge of old script will be tested and you may need professional help to transcribe and/or interpret these documents.
3. A number of these sources have been compiled, transcribed and published in Flemish (see Appendix C for more details on how to access these compilations.)
4. You will have to do some research to find where these archives are located: records of a smaller community might be found in the archives of a larger municipality or city and you will have to find out to which larger entity the smaller community reported.

Notwithstanding these difficulties, we think it may be worth your patience, determination and perhaps your money, to explore these archives. We therefore present here a few of these records with a sketch of their history and information on how they possibly can be accessed.

THE ALDERMEN'S BENCH - *SCHEPENBANK*

The daily life of our ancestors in Flanders was controlled by the clerical and the secular authorities. The clergy provided us with rich genealogical data in the parish records from the late 1500s. The secular aspects of people's lives were recorded by municipal institutions, originating in the middle and late Middle Ages. One of the most important civil institutions was the aldermen's bench (schepenbank).

Already during the Carolingian times there were aldermen (schepenen) or *scabini (Latin-* or *échevins* in French)* who were magistrates in the castellanies, manors and villages, serving the counts. They exercised juridical power and handled most financial matters of their community. Their archives include rents, real property sales, inheritances, mortgages, marriages contracts, loans, orphan records, estate inventories (*Staten van Goed),* etc. Often they were called *scabinale acten.*

A number of these records, mainly of larger municipalities, have been filmed by the Family History Library. The city of Kortrijk is a good example: in the *rechterlijke registers* (court records) you will find records from 1442 to 1796. The 91 microfilms not only cover the town of Kortrijk but also the municipalities which were under the jurisdiction of Kortrijk. [21]

---

[21] The hunt can be rewarding: in my search for the Goethals family, I located several orphan acts, and rental and loan agreements dating between 1568 and 1671 which aided me in reconstructing my ancestry and in illustrating their lives. See Jozef J. Goethals, *Goethals Tavernier Vanmaele, The Ancestors of(De Voorouders van) August Goethals (1901-1978) and Elza Tavernier (1908-1995).* Gateway Press Inc. Baltimore MD 2006.

Schepenbank History

Nowhere did towns achieve a greater independence than in the communes of Flanders. The economies of the larger towns of Flanders -- Brugge, Ieper, Gent and Arras -- were closely linked by geography to foreign markets. London and other English ports lay close at hand across the channel. The Rhineland and German towns were located to the east, while Champagne, Burgundy were readily accessible in eastern France, as were Italian cities located beyond the Alps.

Following years of desctruction by the Vikings, trade began to develop in the tenth century. From the twelfth to the fourteenth century, Flanders flourished as a textile manufacturing center with wool imported from England. By the middle of the fourteenth century, Ghent with a population of more than 50,000 was second in size in the region only to Paris.

A growing class of merchants and craftsmen organized guilds for their mutual assistance and enacted laws to regulate business and taxation. Seizing an opportunity to strenghten their feudal authority, the counts granted privileges to the cities, thereby creating a degree of self-governance. During the Carolingian period *schepenen*, or aldermen, served the counts as magistrates, oveerseeing enforcement of the law. The 12 to 13 aldermen soon gained executive power and with it the right to appoint their own members.

This, in turn, created civil rights for the burghers, including the right to own, sell and inherit real property. The cities provided military manpower for the count and assumed the responsibility for their own self-defence. Great changes also occured in the administration of justice. Legal cases formerly settled by duels or "judicia dei" were now presented to *De Vierschaar*, the tribunal of the four (aldermen), for adjudication.

The city of Gent was an example of the growth of these communal institutions. In 1178, Philip of Alsace was the first count to give privileges to the city of Gent. After his death in 1191, the Gentians could obtain from his widow, Mathilde of Portugal, a charter that founded the *Keure of Gent*. (Charter) [22]

The preface of the charter reflects the philosophy of the Gentian burghers: " It is conforming to the law of God and all human reason that the rulers, who have the desire to be honored and served by their subjects, keep stable and intact their rights and customs, because those are not contrary to reason." [23]

These are some of the privileges awarded by the charter:

1. The Gentians owe fidelity and friendship to their sovereign as long as he treats them in accordance with the precepts of justice and reason.

2. The Gentians have the right to fortify their city and private homes as they wish.

3. No edict of the count shall have the force of law without the approval of the magistrate of Gent, and no citizen may be summoned to justice outside the limits of the city without his consent.

4. The government and the administration are entrusted to an Alderman's Bench comprised of

---

[22] The Flemish word *Keure* means "charter". It became the name for the institution which had been created by the charter : *De keure of Gent.*

[23] Fris, *Histoire de Gand,* 21.

12 *schepenen* (aldermen; Latin : *scabini*; French: *échevins*) endowed with the sovereign power to declare peace or war, to assess the death penalty or to order deportation.

5. Military service to the count is limited.

6. Everyone may open a school in the city.

7. No lay person may be bring another person before a church court.

8. An immigrant may become a burgher of the city after one year and one day.

9. Undesirables can be banned from the city limits for a period of time by authority of the aldermen.

10. The functions of these magistrates are perpetual; they themselves must foresee   the vacancies which occur through death or in case they cannot serve.

In 1192, Boudewijn VIII confirmed the charter and added four more articles-- among them new city laws may not be made by the bailiff or the commune without reciprocal approval, and parishes may be allowed to elect their own parish priests. The charter became a source of great prosperity for Gent, which had become the capital of the countship.[24] Similar privileges were granted in Arras in 1194, in Ieper in 1212, in Douai in 1220, in Brugge and Gent in 1228, and in Lille in 1241.

In 1212 Ferdinand of Portugal, together with his wife Joanna of Constantinople, changed the way in which the magistrate was elected and decided that four "wise men" (electors) chosen by him in the four parishes of the city would be in charge of electing the 13 administrators.

In 1228 the same prince reorganized the college of magistrates, which became *the Council of the XXXIX.* The council was divided into three separate and equal groups:

1. Thirteen *schepenen*, (aldermen or magistrates) of the **Keure.**

   The Tribunal of the Keure was given sovereign governance of the city, the administration of general finances and of justice. The aldermen were responsible for legislative resolutions; they had executive power in finances, public works, public safety and order, personnel and population matters, and juridical cases covering criminal and civil law. The first alderman of the Keure functioned as burgomaster.

2. Thirteen *schepenen* of the **Ghedeele** (French: les parchons).

   They handled simple police matters and the inheritance of minors (the Orphan Bench). They also arbitrated minor legal disputes involving contested inheritances, property rights and reconciliations.

3. Thirteen *Vacants* (*French: les vacans*), or the inactive ones.

   These three division alternated each year. In case of death, a new member was chosen by the entire college in the presence of the Great Bailiff of Gent.

---

[24] Arras was the capital before, but Boudewijn VIII had conceded Arras and Artois to king Philip August of France.

City Hall of Gent. Seat of the "Keure"
(Drawing by Gaston Desmet)

Count Guy of Dampierre confirmed all the ancient customs and privileges of the commune in a new *Second Keure of Gent* on 7 April 1297. He instiued, however, a yearly public accounting of their procedures, and gave thereby greater control to the common people. This charter remained the fundamental charter of the city until 1540.

Between 1228 and 1540 the Keure wielded its power in the city. Over the years, the aldermen developed into a cast of their own which did not always have the interest of the count of the common people in mind. They resisted paying the counts and kings for their military expeditions and, as a result, their privileges were sometimes amended or abrogated by their rulers. Feeling all-powerful, they closed their eyes when collegues abused their privileges to the detriment of the "regular" people. The famous Gentian historian Victor Fris called it " the tyranny of the XXXIX who treated the people as serfs."[25] The city suffered under a series of revolts against the counts, and internal fighting among the guilds, aldermen and lower classes was common.

In 1540, emperor Charles V put an end to the revolts of his native rebellious city: he personally came to Gent on 14 February 1540 and abrogated all its privileges. He established a new constitution of 74 articles, and created a new assembly of aldermen with 42 delegates from the seven parishes, chosen by the bailiff. The guilds were reduced from 53 to 21, and the leaders of the city were publicly dishonored. The *Caroline Concession* of 30 April 1540 ended the independent power of the municipality.

---

[25] Fris, *Histoire de Gand*, 35.

The college of the *schepenen* remained as a principal government structure but was now under the direct power and supervision of the empire. This system continued during the rest of the Ancien Régime until 6 July 1794, when the French revolutionaries replaced it with their own administrative system

INVENTORY OF THE ESTATE- *STAAT VAN GOED* AND ORPHAN GUARDIANSHIP- *WEEZERIE*

Another vital source is to be found in **orphan guardianship** in Flanders, a practice which goes back to ca the 13th century. Although time and place reveal differences in its rules and applications , the basic structure remained the same for centuries.

At the death of one the parents, children up to 25 years of age were considered to be minor orphans. Within 14 days to 6 weeks, depending on the location, a request for guardianship had to be submitted to the aldermen of the jurisdiction to which the deceased belonged. This could be a seigniory or a town. Failure to do so could incur a penalty.

An inventory of all personal property and real estate, including all debts and credits of the family, was compiled. In Flemish, this document was called a *Staat van Goed* or a *Boedelbeschrijving*. In some jurisdictions this documents is listed under a different name: for eample, the Kasselrij of Ieper called it a *Doodhalm*. A short version of the *Staat van Goed* was called a *weesact* (orphan act) and it listed only the goods given to the orphans following division of the inheritance. It is important to obtain both documents, if at all possible.

Two guardians were appointed, usually one from each side of the family: the *voogd paterneel - VP* (paternal guardian) and the *voogd materneel- VM* (maternal guardian). Although the surviving parent retained care of the children, the management of the property was the responsibility of the guardians who were required to submit a yearly report of their management to the aldermen.

Many **indices of** those **inventories** have been published. A draw back is that they are published in Flemish, but they follow a standard pattern and could be understood by some one who does not know the language. If you know the place and year of a deceased person and a number of your ancestors died in that location, it might be worthwhile going to the website of the local VVF and see if they have publications of inventories and order the publication. (See the websites p.65)

The indices usually contain the following data:

1. The place and the catalogue number of the volume, with the *folio(s)* where the *staat van goed* may be found. It was customary to number only one side of the sheet, namely the page on the right side, not the reverse side. Thus, for example, Vol. 923/53, refers to the numbered page, also named *recto,* whereas the reverse side is referred to as *53 v•* or *verso;*

2. The *staet van* (estate of) followed by the name/maiden name of the deceased, the parents, and sometimes grandparents;

3. Next there may be the word *poorter* or *poorteresse* (burgher of burgheress); if the person was not a poorter, the word *non-poorter* or *gediede* or *gedijde*, or *vrijlaet*, coud be found here. (More

about poorters in the next section);

4. The place and date of death;

5. The name of the spouse, whether surviving or deceased (indicated by +), usually followed by his/her parents;

6. The children or other heirs; if a married son was predeceased, his children; if a married daughter was predeceased, her husband and children;

7. The guardians, indicated by *VP, voogd paterneel* (paternal guardian); *VM, voogd materneel* (maternal guardian); the guardian's name may be followed by a word indicating his relationship (*schoonbroer,* brother-in-law; *broer,* brother; *nonkel,* uncle...) and his place of residence.

8. Sometimes this is followed by the letters CA, i.e. *contract antenuptiaal* (prenuptial contract)

9. Finally, the word *acte* (act or record) and the date of its draft.

Here is an example of one of those published indexes:

902/193v• - 939/174

Staet van Gillis DENYS fs Gillis, poorter van R(oeselare), overleden in october 1694, man van Christijne VERELST fa Jan. Kinderen: Jacobus; Lodewijk. V.P. Hendrick Pardou; V.M. Pieter Verelst. Het kind van Gillis en Martine vande Vijvere fa Guillaume, nl. Marie Anna. V.M.Guillaume vande Vijvere d'oude. Acte 9.5.1695

Estate of Gillis Denys, son of Gillis, burgher of Roeselare, deceased in october 1694, husband of Christijne Verelst, daughter of Jan. Children: Jacobus, Lodewijk. Paternal guardian Hendrick Pardou; Maternal guardian Pieter Verelst. The child of Gillis and Martine vande Vijvere, daughter of Guillaume, namely Marie Anna; Maternal guardian Guillaume vande Vijvere the elder. Act 9.5.1695

Other details are usually not provided in the indices. To obtain a copy of the **whole record**, one must go to the place where the register is kept - usually the archives- indicating *Weeserie* or *staat van goed,* the catalogue number and folio.

The original document is usually divided into several parts:

- the introduction naming the parties involved
- a memo about the presence or absence of a prenuptial contract and who drafted it
- the *baeten* (benefits- or credits) consisting of all real estate, owned or rented, and movables and cash on hand
- the *passieve schulden en lasten* (debts and charges)
- the balance sheet between the credits and debits
- description of how the property will be divided
- names of the registrar and the *deelslieden* (people assigned to perform the actual division of the property)

The division of estates can also be found in the **notary public acts** of larger municipalities and the neighboring towns. The 264 notary public microfilms of the city of Gent, for example, contain records from 1548 to 1831 (next to their aldermen's acts from 1339 to 1788 and their guardianship records from 1349 to 1795!)

🐏 In your Family History Library search of any town, always see if there are *guardianship records, orphan acts, court records and notary public acts.*(For compilations of local aldermen's records, see the VVF publications and how to access them on p.64-65.)

TAX LISTS - *PENNINGSKOHIEREN*

A unique ancient source which may help you reconstruct your family's possessions are the tax lists of the late 1500s or the *penningskohieren.*

On 21 March 1569, Alva (see history) imposed two taxes on the Flemish population: a one-time *100ste penning* (100th penny), 1% on all goods and property; and a "permanent" tax of the *10de penning* (10th penny), 10 % on all sales of personal property, and the *20ste penning* (20th penny) , 5 % on all real estate property. In each town the clerks made an inventory of all renters and owners of land and houses. The renters had to pay the 5%; the owners who worked their own property had to pay taxes on the products of the land.

At first, the taxes were not really collected, but on 31 July 1571 Alva made the tax collection mandatory and the payments started to arrive in August of that year. Because of pressure by the population and general opposition to the new practice, Alva stopped the tax collection in 1572, but the practice still continued until well into 1584.

The result of this tax imposition is a host of *penningscolhieren* of a large number of Flemish towns, villages and manors, which are located in the archives. The orginals are hard to decipher and require expert knowledge of ancient Flemish script. Patient local genealogists, however, have transcribed many of the tax lists and published them. The records provide a detailed description of all properties, their owners and renters in a certain location and the taxes that were assessed. If you are lucky enough to find that a transcription has been made of the town where your ancestors lived, you may be able to reconstruct their financial picture![26]

Most of these publications - in old Flemish- are available at local VVF Centers and libraries but you may need a translator to help you out.

"BURGHERS" AND "NONRESIDENT BURGHERS"
POORTERS EN BUITEN-POORTERS

The exact origin of the burgher ship is unknown, but it coincided with the development of the cities in Flanders in the 10th and 11th centuries. People moved from the rural areas to the city to free themselves from serfdom of the feudal lords. After living one year and one day in the city, the rural feudal lord had no further claim on them because they were now burghers, *poorters.* The term *poorter (Masc)* and *poorteresse (Fem.)* were not used in every Flemish city: the term *keurebroer* (charter brother) and *keurezuster* (charter sister) were used in the city and castellany of Veurne. Within other territories, such as the *Brugse Vrije* (Franc of Brugge), the term *laat* and *vrijlaat* were the equivalent of *poorter.*

---

[26] See for example: Luc Neyt, *Cohier vander Stede van Thielt binnen vanden XX⁰ penninck, 1571,* VVF Tielt, 2003.

The contract between city and individual and the conditions for becoming a burgher differed from city to city. One could become a burgher by birth or by marriage to a burgher or burgheress. It was also possible to buy burgher ship by registering and paying a certain fee, which may differ from town to town. New poorters were registered in the city accounts (*stadsrekeningen*). Often special lists, *poorterslijsten*, were drafted. Many of these have been published and can be a valuable help in reconstructing your ancestry line.

There were important privileges connected to burgher ship: it gave access to certain city jobs (alderman, e.g.); it gave the right to conduct a business in the city (butcher, brewer); burghers were freed from paying certain taxes and road tolls; their goods could not be confiscated by the king; their house was inviolable; they could appeal to the aldermen's bench (schepenbank) in juridical matters; the Orphan Chamber automatically arranged for the guardianship of orphans and their accounting to the city's aldermen; and most importantly, the feudal lord could not claim the best part of a burgher's inheritance.

An individual, man or woman, could also become a *buitenpoorter*(outer burgher or nonresident burgher) of a city without residing there while benefitting from the same privileges. So while living in Tielt, one could be a outside burgher of Kortrijk, as long as a yearly fee was paid.

This outside burghership started in Kortrijk in 1324. By 1398 there were 7,753 outside burghers of Kortrijk. In 1577 the largest number of outside burghers was recorded (13,002) spread among towns like Deinze, Harelbeke, Menen, and Tielt, which counted 781 outside burghers. Since 1639 the so-called "blue books"(blauwe boeken) recorded the yearly payments of the outside burghers.

Burgher ship provided a certain social standing in the community. This does not mean that it was reserved for the 'high society": next to the parish priest and the noble, there were many trades people, farmers and regular folks who were burghers. The main purpose of becoming a burgher or outside burgher was to protect the family and its possessions.

FLEMISH SURNAMES AND CHRISTIAN NAMES

We take it for granted that every person has a first name and a surname. This has not always been the case, and family names were common only from the Middle Ages on. Earlier, the Romans had used second and third names to set apart their family relationships: Scipio "Africanus" wanted to be remembered for his African exploits; Gaius Julius Caesar showed that he was from the Julius family.

In Flanders before the 12th century surnames and nicknames were usually not inherited. They helped to identify a person but died with him. They came in a variety of forms. They could describe a person's appearance: Pieter de Corte (*kort*= short) or Jan de Langhe (*lang*= tall). They could record an incident or exploit: Cornelis de Messevechter (knife fighter) or Count Baldwin "with the Axe". They could indicate a connection with another person: Pieter Jan's Zoone (Pieter, the son of Jan) or Pieter Dejonge (*jong* = the young one) in contrast with Pieter " de ouden" (*oud* = old). They could denote someone's residence (Augustijn *van Gent*) or occupation (Hendrick *de Brouwer* - the brewer). Genealogical research is complicated by the fact that names did not always pass on from father to son. Hendrick "the brewer" may have been the son of Jan "the carpenter."

The custom of having an inherited name originated with royal and noble families in the feudal Middle Ages. These families began adding the name of their estate or feudal fief to their first name. One of the earliest examples is Geoffrey IV of " Plantagenet" in early England. Most of the nobility followed the example of kings and counts, the bourgeoisie aped them, and soon the lower classes followed suit. Surnames gradually became a necessity because of the population explosion and the importance of keeping accurate records of fief holders and taxation.

Family names became a custom in Flanders between 1250 and 1300. Italy used surnames in the twelfth century. A surname now passed from father to son, but it was easy to change it or to spell it in a variety of ways. It was not until France's occupation of Flanders in 1795 that one needed a juridical procedure to change the family name.

Flemish family names come from an incredible variety of sources.

The oldest way of "creating" a family name was to add *"zoon van"* (son of) to a christian name: Jan, zoon van Willem, became Jan Willemszoon, or Jan Willemsen, and later simply Jan Willems.[27] Examples of *patronymic surnames* are: Huybrechts (Hubertus), Dierckens (Dirk), Daneels (Daniel), Pieters (Pieter), Cornelissen (Cornelis).

A wide variety of surnames are derived from *places* ; from the four cardinal points (van Noort, van West; *"van"* -from) to countries, regions and cities (van Brabant, Lombaerts - Lombardy in Italy-, van Melle, van Weezemaele, van Ackerghem).

A very rich category is *seigniories, hamlets, estates and farms*, and everything that was a part

---

[27] Names derived from the father are called *patronymic*; when they are derived from the mother's name they are *metronymic* or *matronymic*.

of them, grew on them or lived on them: Vandecasteele (*kasteel*=castle); Verhoeven (*hoeve, hove* =farm), sometimes with "uit de" -from, as in Uyttenhove; Vermeulen (*molen, meulen* = mill); van de Capelle (*kapel*=chapel); Ackerman (*akker*= cultivated land); van Hecke (*hek*=fence); Vanderheyden (*heide*=heather); Vandenbossche (*bosh*= forest); Verhaeghe (*haag*= hedge); van der Gracht (*gracht*=ditch) ; van Dycke (*dyk*= dike or ditch); Opdebeek (*beek*= brook). Even Flemish rivers were included: Scheldeman and van Overschelde (Scheldt); Vermandere (Mander); Verbrugge (*brug*= bridge) and Vandewalle (*wal*= embankment).

Animals were inspiration for family names: De Beer (bear), Dewulf (wolve) and Devos (fox). The nickname Devos may have been given because of a person's sly character or Nachtegaele (nightingale) because of his musical talent.

Very common were names derived from a *trade or profession*. A few trades: Decasemaeker (*kaas*=cheese); Devleeshouwer (*vlees-houwer*=meat-cutter"); Timmerman and Carpentier (carpenter); de Pottere (pottery maker); Demets (*metselaar*=mason). Professions; De Meestere (*meester*=master, indicates education); De Schrijvere (*schrijven*=to write); de Raedt (*raad*=council); de Ruddere (*ridder*= knight) and Nobels (noble).

Finally there are names that connote a *physical or character trait*. Bruneel or Debruyne(*bruin*= brown) suggests hair color; de Langhe (*lang*= tall) and de Corte (*kort*=short) height; Bultinck (*bult*=hunchback) and den Dooven (*doof*=deaf) a physical disability. Character traits could be positive or negative: Goeghebeur (*goed-gebuur*=good neighbor) or Quaghebeur (*kwaad-gebuur*= bad neighbor); Devroe(de) (*vroed*=wise); de Lodder (*loeder*=rascal) and Dezeure (*zuur*=sour, unpleasant).

Christian Names

It has been a 2000 year custom to give a baptismal name to the child or adult to be baptized. For ages the Catholic Church required the name of a saint, or of a virtue.
(Charity, Felicitas, Deodatus- "gift of God").[28] After the Council of Trent all parishes were required to record baptisms, and most first names were latinized. Some people would keep the Latin version of their name in daily life. Orphan Chamber and Aldermen's records show that most people used the Flemish or French versions of their baptismal name. A second or middle name was mostly unknown before 1750, but became common by 1850.

To facilitate the name identification, we are including a list of the most common names in three languages.

Latin	Flemish	French
Women's Names		
Adriana	Naentgen	Adrienne
Aegidia	Ghelyne	

---

[28] This custom was abrogated by the new Code of Canon Law (canon 855). The saint's name is no longer required, " as long as the name is not alien or offensive to Christian sensibilities".

Anna	Tanneken	Anne
	Calleken	
Catharina	Katlyne	Catherine
Cecilia	Ceelken	Cecile
Christina	Christyntken	Christine
Elisabetta	Betgen, Liesbeth	Elisabeth
Francisca	Francyn	Françoise
Jacoba	Jacomyne	Jacqueline
	Jacquemyne	
Joanna	Janneken	Jeanne
Judoca	Joosyne	Justine
	Joosyntken	
Livina	Livyne	Livine
Magdalena	Leen	Madeleine
Maria	Mayken	Marie
Margarita	Magriet	Marguerite
Martina	Martynken	Martine
Petronilla	Peryntgen, Neele	Petronelle
	Pieryntgen	
Pharailda	Veerle	Pharilde

Men's Names

Adrianus	Adriaan	Adrien
Arnoldus	Arendt	Arnaud
Augustinus	Augustijn	Augustin
Balduinus	Boudewyn	Baudouin
Carolus	Karel	Charles
Christianus	Chris	Chrétien
Christophorus	Stoffel, Kristoffel	Christophe
Donatus	Donaas	Donatien
Donatianus		
Egidius	Gillis	Gilles
Eustachius	Staes	Eustache
Franciscus	Franchois,Francyn	François
Georgius	Joris	George
Gerardus	Geeraert	Gérard
Guilielmus	Willem	Guillaume
Henricus	Hendrick	Henri
Hieronymus	Hieronymus	Jerome
	Jeroen	
Ignatius	Ignaas	Ignace

Jacobus	Jacob,Copken	Jacques
Joannes	Jan	Jean
	Hans, Hanneken	
Joannes Baptista	Jan Baptist	Jean Baptiste
Josephus	Joseph, Jozef	Joseph
Judocus	Joos	Josse
Laurentius	Lauweryns	Laurent
Livinus	Lieven,Livyn	Liévin
Ludovicus	Lodewyk, Lowys	Louis
Martinus	Maarten	Martin
Mattheus	Mattheeus, Thys	Matthieu
Michael	Michiel	Michel
Nicolaus	Niklaas,Nicolaas	Nicolas
Paulus	Pauwels	Paul
Petrus	Pieter,Pierken	Pierre
Zegerus	Seger	Sohier,Siger

STATE ARCHIVES IN FLANDERS
(Rijksarchieven)

When your search for your ancestors has exhausted all the sources available in the U.S., you might have to travel to Belgium to advance or complete your search. Belgium has a well-organized and rich archival system on the municipal as well as on the national/federal level.

For information on municipal archives, you can find on the **Belgium-Roots Project** website a list of 3,000 municipalities and place-names with their administrative districts (arrondissements) and provinces. Many of the municipalities have websites where you can find what they keep in their archival collections and how you can contact them.

The *Rijksarchieven* or "State" or "National Archives" are the most important archival sources.[29] Each state archive holds sources covering the administrative district in which it is located, containing records on castellanies, aldermen's benches, municipalities, private family archives, parish councils, monasteries, hospitals, etc. Many have an extended collection of maps and property records. They also have copies of Family History Library microfilms of the parish registers of the district.

---

[29] To stay within the scope of this book,we will discus the State Archives of the Flemish provinces only: West-and East Flanders, Antwerp, Limburg and Flemish Brabant.

On 2 June 2006, new rules for access and protocol for all state archives were approved. [30] To have access to the archives you will need to purchase an admittance card. These cards are issued for a year and give access to all state archives in Belgium. An alternative is a card for one week issued for seven consecutive days, but your access is limited to the archives where the card is issued. Students at universities and other institutions of higher learning can get a 50% discount.

At your first visit, you will need to register and an I.D. - or a passport for foreigners- is required. If you are already in possession of a card, you just have to register. The card will be kept at the reception desk until you leave the premises.

The reading rooms have a lot of materials accessible as "self-service", although nothing can leave the premises. If you need to request original archival pieces, the archivists will assist you. In some of the archives a computerized *Archeion* system will help with your request; in other cases individual request forms are needed for each piece you want to study. The handling of archival pieces is subject to strict rules. There are limitations and guidelines concerning the copying of materials. Photographing documents with digital cameras has been temporarily approved, but the when, how, and what are subject to strict guidelines.

Opening hours of the State Archives are:
Tuesdays to Fridays: 8.30 A.M. to 4.30 P.M.
 Saturdays: 8.30 A.M. to 12.00; 1.00 P.M. to 4.00 P.M.
In July-August: closed on Mondays and Saturdays and during the lunch period 12.00-1.00

The *Rijksarchieven* - State Archives in the Flemish Provinces

Algemeen Rijksarchief - General State Archives
Ruisbroeckstraat 2
1000 Brussel
Tel (32) 02/ 513.76.80
Fax (32) 02/ 513.76.81
Algemeen.Rijksarchief@arch.be

Rijksarchief te Antwerpen - State Archives of Antwerp
Door Verstraeteplein 5
2018 Antwerpen
Tel and Fax (32) 03/ 236.73.00
Rijksarchief.Antwerpen@arch.be

Rijksarchief te Beveren - State Archives of Beveren
Kruibekesteenweg 39/1
9120 Beveren
Tel (32) 03 750.29.77   Fax (32) 03/ 750.29.70
Rijksarchief.Beveren@arch.be

---

[30] See *Genealogie en Heraldiek in Vlaanderen*, jg 4, nr. 4, July 2006, 209-217.

The state archives of Beveren, in addition to functioning as state archives for the disctrict of Dendermonde, serves as repository of all national/federal archives *for all the Flemish provinces* since 1976. All the original parish registers and civil registers of the Flemish provices are kept there but cannot be accessed.

Beveren serves also as a genealogical center where microfilms of parish registers, civil registers, and other genealogical sources (populations registers, aldermen's acts, orphan acts, etc) of the district of Dendermonde and Gent, are available. Since July 2001 Family History Library microfilm copies of all parish and civil records of all Flemish provinces are at hand.

Rijksarchief te Brugge- State Archives of Brugge
Academiestraat 14-28
8000 Brugge
Tel (32) 050/ 33.72.88
Fax (32) 050/ 61.09.18
Rijksarchief.Brugge@arch.be
The archives of Brugge contain archives of public institutions of the administrative districts of Brugge, Veurne and Ieper in West-Flanders. It also holds the archives of the Ancien Regime within the province of West-Flanders and its local institutions (cities, castellanies, manors, aldermen's benches, etc.) and its religious entities (diocese, abbeys, monasteries, etc). In 1996 their entire collection of maps and plans was placed on microfilm and is available to the public.

Rijksarchief te Gent- State Archives of Gent
Geeraard de Duivelstraat 1
9000 Gent
Tel (32) 09/ 225.13.38
Fax (32) 09/ 225.52.01
Rijksarchief.Gent@arch.be
Gent prides itself on owning the records of the central government's institutions of the Countship of Flanders and the high courts (*Raad van Vlaanderen* -Council of Flanders) (to 1796) and the provincial government of East Flanders (to 1870).

Rijksarchief te Hasselt- State Archives of Hasselt
Bampslaan 4
3500 Hasselt
Tel (32) 011/ 22.17.66
Fax (32) 011/ 23.40.46
Rijksarchief.Hasselt@arch.be
The archives of Hasselt contain the records of the area presently covering the province of Limburg.

Rijksarchief te Kortrijk - State Archives of Kortrijk
Guido Gezellestraat 1
8500 Kortrijk

Tel (32) 056/ 21.32.68
Fax (32) 056/ 20.57.42
Rijksarchief.Kortrijk@arch.be

Rijksarchief te Leuven- State Archives of Leuven(Louvain)
College van Villers, Vaartstraat 24, Leuven
Tel (32) 016/31.49.54
Fax (32) 016/31.49.61
Rijksarchief.Leuven@ arch.be
The archives cover the records of the province of Flemish Brabant.

Rijksarchief te Ronse- State Archives of Ronse
Vanhovestraat 45
9600 Ronse
Tel and Fax (32) 055/ 21.19.83
Rijksarchief.Ronse@arch.be
    The archives cover the administrative district of Oudenaarde. It also functions as the municipal archives of Ronse and Geeraardsbergen.

APPENDIX C

THE FLEMISH ASSOCIATION FOR FAMILY HISTORY
VLAAMSE VERENIGING VOOR FAMILIEKUNDE (V.V.F.)

    The largest genealogical society in Belgium is the **V.V.F.- Vlaamse Vereniging voor Familiekunde - Flemish Association for Family History.** Founded in 1964, this society has many local branches spread over all Flemish provinces in Belgium. Its magazine is the *Vlaamse Stam.*

    A few years ago, an umbrella organization, recognized by the Flemish Ministry of Culture, brings together the most important genealogical organizations in Flanders. This umbrella organization is called **Samenwerkingsverband Vlaamse Verenigingen voor Familiekunde (SVVF)**[31] (Collaboration Link Flemish Associations of Genealogy). It operates four major documentation centers. Each center has an extensive library of primary and secondary sources. Use of the libraries is for members of the VVF but you can get a visitor's card for a nominal fee.

    - Nationaal VVF-Centrum voor Familiegeschiedenis (The National VVF Center for Family History), Van Heyenbeeckstraat 3, 2170 Merksem (Nationaal VVF-Centrum voor Familiegeschiedenis). Tel. 03 646 99 88 - Fax: 03 644 46 20.

---

[31] Website < http://www.svvf.be>

http://users.pandora.be/vvfmerksem

The center contains 20,000 books, among them 2,300 family histories, 1,900 compiled sources and 1,560 local histories. The center has catalogued 600,000 death memorial cards and 350,000 death memorial letters. [32]

- Vlaams Centrum voor Genealogie en Heraldiek (Flemish Centrum for Genealogy and Heraldics,), Kronevoordestraat 2a, 8610 Kortemark-Handzame. Tel. 051 56 74 79.
http://www..vcgh.be
The Handzame center has a shadow archive of parish records on micro-fiche; population census of the 17th, 18th and 19th centuries; burgher lists, estate inventories, etc.

-Oost-Vlaams Documentatiecentrum (East Flemish Documentation Center), Brusselsesteenweg 393, 9090 Melle. Tel. 09 252 26 47. (Oost-Vlaams Documentatiecentrum).

- Provinciaal VVF-Centrum voor Familiegeschiedenis Oostende (Provincial VVF Center for Family History Oostende), Kan. Dr. L. Colenstraat 6, 8400 Oostende. Tel. 059 80 93 44.
http://users.skynet.be/fa055068
Besides its extensive library of primary and secondary works, the library holds a collection of all parish record indexes for all of West-Flanders; 723,000 death memorial cards and 951,000 death memorial letters.

Two sister organizations within the VVF are worth mentioning: *Genealogy and Computer* and *the Heraldic College*.

In 1984 the VVF founded **VVF- Genealogie en Computer** as a branch of the association. They report in the magazine *Genealogie & Heraldiek in Vlaanderen*. Their "Ariadne on Line" website carries 9.5 millions data blocks. The site is continuously expanded with Gedcom contributions of its membership. The website is only accessible to members of the association using a bi-monthly changing password.

The Heraldic College **(Heraldisch College)** was founded in 1973 to propagate and popularize the use family coats of arms in Flanders. They have registered and publicized hundreds of family shields. [33]
The use of family shields is commonly attributed to nobility. From the 13th century on, however, the use of shields spread to all levels of society: clergy, tradesmen, and well-to-do families. This gave rise to *corporate heraldry*: cities and towns, universities, guilds and other institutions obtained their own coats of arms.
In Flanders, the use of family coats of arms was interrupted from 1795 to 1815 because the French revolutionaries saw them as signs of nobility and feudalism. Presently, you can register an

---

[32] The custom of sending Death memorial letters at the death of a family member is a very Belgian one. The letters provide the genalogists with information on the deceased and his extended family.

[33] Their website is (in Flemish) : < http://users.skynet.be/sky60754/vvf/vvfheraldcollege.htm>

old coat of arms if you can prove, through archival evidence, that one of your distant ancestors carried the coat of arms. One can apply to the Heraldic College for a new coat of arms which can be based on name etymology, family trades or professions, origins, etc. The creation of such a weapon is subject to stringent rules established by the College. If approved, the carrier will receive an official *wapenbrief* (weapon letter) and the shield will be made public in the *Vlaamse Stam.*

If you know some Flemish and you are serious about finding out more about your ancestors, it is recommended that you join the VVF. Purchasing a good Flemish dictionary might not be a bad idea. The yearly membership of 52 Euros gives you access to their publications *De Vlaamse Stam* and *Genealogie & Heraldiek in Vlaanderen* (started in 2003)[34] and also free access to their resource centers. All previous issues of *de Vlaamse Stam* can be purchased on CDRom.

---

[34] In the Nov-Dec 2006 issue of *Genealogy & Heraldiek* is was announced that the magazine would no longer be published in its present form in 2007.

Provincial Branch of *Antwerpen* (no website)
 Regional Branch *Antwerpen*: **<http://users.belgacom.net/vvfantwerpen>**
 Regional Branch the *Kempen* : **<http://users.pandora.be/vvfkempen>**
 Regional Branch *Mechelen*: **<http://www.vvfmechelen.be>**
Provincial Branch *Brussels* Hoofdstedelijk Gewest (Brussels Capital): **<www.vvf-brussel.be>**
Provincial Branch *Limburg* (no website)
Provincial Branch *West-Vlaanderen* (West-Flanders) **<http://www.vvfwestvlaanderen.be>**
 Regional Branch *Brugge* : **<http://users.skynet.be/geneadub/index.htm>**
 Regional Branch *Kortrijk*:
  <http://users.pandora.be/johan.roelstraete/vvffiles/vvfkortrijk.html>
 Regional Branch *Oostende* : **<http://users.skynet.be/fa055068>**
 Regional Branch *Tielt*: **<http://up.to/vvftielt>**
 Regional Branch *Westhoek*: **<www.vvf-westhoek.be>**
 Regional Branch *Westkust*: **<http:/www.vvf-westkust.be>**
Provincial Branch *Oost-Vlaanderen* (East-Flanders) :**<www.vvfovl.be>**
 Regional Branch *Aalst* **<www.vvfaalst.be>**
 Regional Branch *Deinze* : **<http://www.vvfdeinze.be>**
 Regional Branch *Dendermonde* **<www.vvf-dendermonde.be>**
 Regional Branch *Gent* **<www.vvfgent.be>**
 Regional Branch *Land van Waas*: **<www.vvflandvanwaas.be>**
 Regional Branch *Meetjesland* **<http://vvfmeetjesland.cjb.net>**
 Regional Branch *Vlaamse Ardennen* (Flemish Ardennes) :
  <www.31.brinkster.com/vvfvlaamseard>
Provincial Branch *Vlaams Brabant* (Flemish Brabant)
  <http://home.scarlet.be/~jdebeurm/index.htm>
 Regional Branch *Aarschot*: **<http://scarlet.be/~jdebeurm/Bestaarschot.htm>**
 Regional Branch *Dilbeek* **<http://members.tripod.com//vvfdilbeek>**
 Regional Branch *Huldenberg* **<www.huisterdijle.be>**
 Regional Branch *Leuven* **<http://scarlet.be/~jdebeurm/Bestleuven.htm>**
 Regional Branch *Tienen* **<http://scarlet.be/~jdebeurm/Besttienen.htm>**

 The reason we are giving here a complete list of provincial and regional branches of the VVF is that local chapters publish many transcriptions and compilations of original sources, such as parish records, orphan acts, legal documents, etc. Even if your knowledge of the Flemish language is limited, these sources could save you a lot of time and effort! The perusal and analysis of the original documents have already been done! At a certain point in your research, it might be worthwhile seeing what is avalable at the local chapters of the VVF and purchase some of these publications. The websites of the VVF chapters usually provide a list of their publications (*publikaties* or *uitgaven)*. If your research brings you to Belgium, you can access these published sources at the VVF centers.

We are citing here one example that illustrates how important these publications can be. Suppose your family originates from the area of Roeselare in West-Flanders. VVF Roeselare has a list of 82 publications on Roeselare and surrounding towns. Here are some publications on the town of Roeselare:

Publ. 67: Alfabetical tables on the 19th century parish registers

Publ. 68: Inheritance registrations of the Registers Office Roeselare 1830-1910

Publ. 70: Legal acts of the seigniory "Den Hazelt" 1609-1619

West-Flemish pedigrees (5 volumes)[35]

Publ. 33: Population Beveren-Roeselare anno 1786

Publ. 18-26: Staten van Goed-Doodhalmen[36] - Inheritance registrations from 1532 to 1796

You will have to decide if a purchase is worth it. If you happen to have relatives in Belgium, you could ask them to check the publication (all publications of VVF members are sent to the National VVF Center in Merksem) and have copies made of the relevant pages.

APPENDIX D

CURRENCY AND LAND MEASUREMENTS

Assessing the value of money in a particular period of history is an almost impossible task. Until the French Revolution, when the French *franc* was used as currency, the pound system was common, although a variety of pounds were widely used: the *pond groot vlaams (pound grand flemish)* (Lb gvl); the *pond parisis (Lb par)* (Paris pound); the *pond grooten Brabants (Lb gBr)* (Brabant pound); the *pond Artois* or *gulden (Lb art)* (pound of Artois or the guilder); and the *pond tournois (Lb ts)* (pound of Tournai). Not all these pounds had a similar value: the Lb gVl, for example, was 12 pound parisis.

1 *pond* (pound) *(lb)* was 20 *schellingen(s)* (shillings*)* or 240 *penningen (p)* (pennies) or *deniers.* One shilling was 12 pennies. *1 gulden* (guilder) or *florin* was 20 *stuivers (st)* or *patards* (5 cent piece).

A few examples of the buying power of a pound in the 16th century may give you an idea of the financial state of some of your ancestors. [37]

The amount 3-12-15 represents 3 pounds, 12 shillings and 15 pennies. Today's value of a pound is estimated at ca $ 135. The president of the *Raad van State* and a member of the Council of Flanders had a yearly income of 1,200 pounds. A skilled worker earned 30 to 45 pounds a year and an unskilled one 17.5 to 30 pounds. The price of one acre of land was 2.5 to 16 pounds depending on its location and the quality of the soil. In Anwerp a small house cost 2.5 to 6.5 pounds and a

---

[35] Some of the pedigrees are available at the Buyse Library of the GSFA in Milines, Ill.

[36] *Doodhalmen* is a word used for acts of inheritance in the castellany of Ieper. The act had to be drafted two weeks after the death of a person and is similar to the *Staat van Goed.*

[37] See Gibert Rogiers, *Het kasteel van Lozer. 350 jaar bezit van de familie della Faille d'Huysse.* (2004).

large one 18 to 100 pounds. The average rent of a house in Brugge was 3 to 15 pounds a year. The price of an ox: 7 pounds; a draught horse: 10 to 19 pounds; a riding horse: 4 to 25 pounds; 100 sheep: 68 pounds. Renting a riding horse for one day cost 2 shillings and 6 pennies.

Some every day necessities: a tub of butter: 6 pounds 10 shilling.; a barrel of Rhinewine: 30 pounds; a white bread: 2 pennies; a banquet: 2 pounds 5 shilling. For a pair of shoes you paid 6 shilling; boots: 1-1-8 and a hat was 8 shilling. You could be buried in a first class coffin for 2-13-4. Some items for the well-to-do: a harpsicord for 8-6-8; a gold chain for 20 to 40 pounds; a return trip to London cost 9 pounds 2 shilling and to Venice 14 to 32 pounds.

LAND MEASUREMENTS

Land measurements during the Old Regime in Flanders are a complicated matter because no standard measurements were applied throughout the country. When you have located a family property in a certain town, it will be necessary to find out in what jurisdiction the town was located in order to have an idea of the acreage. Each general area, and sometimes each individual town or village, had its own surface measurements.

An important source for identifying these land systems is the work of P. Vandewalle, *Oude maten, gewichten en muntstelsels in Vlaanderen, Brabant en Limburg.* (Old measurements, weights and money systems in Flanders, Brabant and Limburg). [38] The book was published in HTML format in 1999 by VVF Genealogy and Computer with permission of the author.[39] Although the information is in Flemish, the data can easily be figured out.

In the Kortrijk region, for example, the most common land measurement was the *roede.* A large square roede was 35.42 m2 or 0.09 acres; a small roede was 8.86 m2. 100 roede was a *vierendeel* (quarter part) and 4 vierendeel was a *bunder* (14,168 m2 or 3.6 acres). Sometimes land is also measured in *100-lants,* representing 25 roeden or 885,5 m2. In Brabant, on the other hand, a roede was 14.85 m2 and a bunder was 900 roeden or 13.365 m2.

---

[38] Belgisch Centrum voor landelijke geschiedenis, publikaie nr 82, Gent 1984.
[39] www.svvf.be. Go to 'hulpwetenschappen' (auxiliary sciences) -- ' maten en gewichten' (measurements and weights) for a complete lay out.

APPENDIX E

GLOSSARY OF FLEMISH, FRENCH AND LATIN TERMS

FLEMISH

A

aanplakking: publication, notification
aanverwant: related (by marriage)
achterleen: lien dependent on another lien
achternaam: surname
acte :act or record
afkondiging: proclamation, publication (of banns)
afschrift: copy of an original record
agierend als: acting as
aldaer: there
alhier: here
ambtenaar: an official
ante-nuptiaal: pre-nuptial
arrondissement: district

B

baljuw: bailiff
Bamis: term related to St. Bavo of Gent, celebrated on October 1. On this date renters paid their rents.
baten (baeten): credits (used in opposition to *schulden:* debts)
begraafplaats: burial place
begrafenis: burial
begraven: buried
beide: both
belasting: taxes
beroep: profession
bevolkingsregister: population register
bidprentje: death memorial card
borgsteller: guarantor
bloedverwant(schap): blood relation(ship)
broer: brother

broederschap: confraternity
bruyd(bruid): bride
bruydegom: bridegroom
beletsel: impediment
boedel: property
boedelbeschrijving: property inventory
buitenpoorter: non-resident burgher
bunder: a landmeasure (14,168 sq.meters; 3.6 acres)
burgemeester: mayor
burgerlijke stand: civil registry
burgerrecht: civil law

C

canoniek recht: church law
cateilen: personal property
cijns: groundrent payable to the lord
cijnsgrond: part of the property of a manor or lien
cognaat: blood relation on the mother's side
cohieren (kohieren) : lists of taxpayers and their obligations
comparant: the person appearing
costume: common law

D

deelvoogd : temporary guardian
denombrement: act describing a lien and the responsibilities of the lienholder and vassal
dis(ch): care of the poor
dochter: daughter
doodhalm: see *staat van goed*
doodsbrief: death memorial letter
doodsprentje, doodsantje : death memorial card
doopheffer: godparent
doopnaam: first name given at baptism
doopsel: baptism
dorp: village

E

echtgenoot (echtgenote): husband (wife)
echtscheiding: divorce

eergisteren: the day before yesterday
erfdeel, erfenis: inheritance
erfgenaam: heir
erfgerechtigde: the person who has the right to inheritance

G

geboorte: birth
geboortig, geboren: born
gebuur : neighbor
gecompareerd: appeared (before)
gedelegeerde ambtenaar: delegated official
gediede, gedijde: town inhabitant lacking the privileges of a burgher (Lat. *foraneus*)
gehuwd: married
gematigde schepen: authorized alderman
gemeente: town
gemeentehuis: town hall
geteekend: signed
getrouwd: married
getuige: witness
gezin: household, family
gisteren : yesterday
grafschrift: epitaph
griffie: court archives
grondbelasting: property taxes

H

handtekening: signature
heden : today, presently
heerlijkheid: manor
houder/ houderigghe: the surviving spouse in a marriage
hoir (oir): direct descendant
huis (huys): house
huisvrouw(huysvrouw): house wife
huwelijk: marriage
huwelijksbijlagen: dossier of supporting documents to be presented before a civil marriage
huwelijksbeletsel: marriage impediment
(in)huwelijk vereenigt: united in marriage

J

(ten) jare: in the year
jongman: unmarried man
jonge dochter: unmarried young woman

K

kadaster: land registry
kasselrij: castellany (an administrative subdivision of the County of Flanders)
kavel: parcel, lot
kavelen: subdivide
kerkhof: cemetery
kerkrecht: church law
keure: name of the Gentian aldermen's bench
kind: child
klapper : index
kwartierstaat: a family tree consisting of all ancestors of one person, both paternal and maternal lines

L

leen: lien or tenure
leenverhef: the relief of a tenure to a new owner; the sum paid at this occasion

M

maand: month
mansgeslacht: of the masculine gender
meerderjarig: major
meter: godmother
middag: midday
middernacht: midnight
minderjarig: minor
moeder: mother

N

naam: surname, family name
nakomeling: descendant
namiddag: afternoon
noen: noon
nonkel: uncle
notaris: notary public

O

officier: officer, employee
onderteekent: signed
overleden: deceased
overlijden: to die; death

P

penningskohier: tax list
peter: godfather
poorter: burgher
poorteres: burgheress
poortersbrief: letter establishing burghership
poorterslijst: burghers list
prisen: estimate

R

rechtbank van eerste aanleg: court of first
    instance
rechterlijke registers: court records
relief: see *leenverhef*
rijksarchief: state archives
roede: part of the castellany of Kortrijk; also a
    land measurement

S

schepen: alderman
schepenbank: aldermen's bench
schoonbroer: brother-in-law
schulden: debts
staat van goed: inventory of all personal
    property and real estate after the death of
    one parent; see *boedelbeschrijving*
staet van...: the estate of
stad: city
stadsrekening: city accounts
sterfhuis: 1.house of deceased person 2. sale by
    auction(personal property and real estate)

T

tante: aunt
tegenwoordig: present
(in) tegenwoordigheid van: in the presence of

telling: census
ten eenre: on the one hand
ten andere : on the other hand
toekomende: future
toestemmende: consenting
trouw: marriage
trouwboekje: marriage booklet

U

uitgaven : publications (also: expenses)
(ten) 6 ure: at six o'clock

V

vader: father
veiling: public auction
vergezeld door: accompanied by
verklaerde: declared
(is-zijn) verschenen: have appeared
vertoond heeft: has presented, shown
verzocht heeft: has requested
verwante: kinship
volkstelling: population census
voltrekken van het huwelijk: performing the
    marriage
voogd paterneel -materneel: paternal guardian,
    maternal
voorlezing: public reading
voormiddag: morning (A.M.)
voornaam: first name
voor ons: for us, in front of us
voorouders: ancestors
vriend: friend
vrouwelijk geslacht: of the feminine gender
vruchtgebruik : usufruct

W

weerbare mannen: fighting men
wees- weeze: orphan- under 25 years of age after
    the death of one of the parents
weeskamer: Orphan Chamber
weezerij: care of the orphans
werkman: laborer

wettelijke passeringen: all legal documents
    drafted by the aldermen's bench
wijlen: late
woonachtig; woonende: living at
woonhuis: house, residence

Z

zegel: seal
zich zelven: his own self (*haar zelven:*her own
    self)
zoon: son
zuster: sister

****
FRENCH

A

acte de décès: death record
acte de mariage: marriage record
acte de naissance: birth record
agé de 5: 5 years old
an: year
Ancien Régime: Old Regime. Term used to
    indicate the period before the French
    occupation of Flanders in 1795
après-midi: afternoon
arrondissement: district
au nom de la loi : in the name of the law

C

ci-dessus: below
citoyen: citizen
commune: town
(est) comparu(e): has appeared
cultivateur: farmer

D

demeurant: living, residing
dresser un act: draft a record

E

écrivain: writer (offical clerk in city hall)
enfant: child

époux- épouse: spouse
état civil: civil registry

F

femme: women, wife
feu (feue): late
fille majeure: (major) daughter- of age
fils majeur: (major) son
fille, fils mineur(e): minor
frère: brother

H

heure: hour
hoir: direct descendant

J

jour: day

L

(après) lecture: after reading

M

maire: mayor
marié: married
maison commune (communale): town or city
    hall
matin: morning
midi: noon
minuit: midnight
mois: month

N

naissance: birth
natif (native): born at
né(e): born
nom: surname
nuit: night

O

officier de l'état civil: officer of the civil registry

P

partis contractants: contracting parties

pièces: official documents
prénom: first name

S

savoir: i.e.
soeur: sister
soir: evening

U

unis par le marriage: united in marriage

****
LATIN

A

ab intestato: inheritance without a testament
ablutus: washed (by baptism)
ab obstetrice baptizatus : baptized by the
    midwife
administratis sacramentis: after administration
    of the sacraments
adstitit: was present
aetatis provectae: at an advanced age
aetatis (suae): at the age of
affidatus (-a): engaged
agnatus, -a: blood relation on the father's side
aliunde: from elsewhere
altera die: the day after
ambo hic nati : both born here
anniculus: only a year old
ante: before
ante diem pridie: the day before yesterday
articulo mortis: at the hour of death
avola=nonna: grandmother
avolo= nonno: grandfather
avus (avia): grandfather (grandmother)

B

baptizatus est (-a): baptized
baptizavi: I have baptized
baptismate necessitatis: emergency baptism
B.M.V.= Beatae Mariae Virginis: of the holy
    virgin Mary

C

causa mortis: cause of death
causidicus: lawyer
celebs, coelebs: unmarried
cemeterio, coemeterio: in the cemetery
circa (circiter): about
cognatus,-a: related
cognomen: surname
commisione pastoris: with permission of the
    pastor
coniugatores: spouses
conjugatus, -a: married
conjugum: of the spouses
conjunx: husband
consensu parentum: with the consent of the
    parents
consuetis ecclesiae sacramentis: with the
    customary sacraments of the church
conversus, -a: convert
coram me et infrascripto pastore: before me and
    the undersigned pastor
coram testibus: before the witnesses
*cum ab illustrissimo ac reverendissimo episcopo
    obtenta dispensatione in bannis*: with a
    dispensation of the banns obtained from the
    illustrious and reverend bishop
cum dispensatione in bannis: with a dispensation
    of the banns

D

declaratus se scribere non posse: declared not
    being able to write
defunctus: deceased
die: on the day
die subsequente: on the following day
dierum: of days
dimidia: and a half
domicillium: place of residence
dispensavit: has given a dispensation
domicella: madam (honorific)
dominus: sir (honorific)

domo propria: in his own house
duxit in matrimonium: married

E

ecclesia: church
eius: his, of him, of her
ejusdem: of the same (month e,g,)
eiusdem loci: of the same place
eodem die: the same day
ex commisione pastoris: instructed by the
    pastor
exeuntium sacramentis munitus: provided with
    the sacraments of the dying
(cum) exequiis summis (majoribus): first class
    burial
(cum) exequiis mediis: second class burial
(cum) exequiis simplicibus: third class burial
extra matrimonium: outside of marriage
extrema unctio: extreme unction
extremis praemunitus: provided with the last
    sacraments
extremis S.R.E.(Sanctae Romanae Ecclesiae)
    sacramentis refectus: strenghtened by the
    last sacraments of the Holy Roman Church

F

facie ecclesiae: in front of the church
factis tribus bannis: after the three banns
femini generis, - sexus: of the female gender
filia: daughter
filiolus, filiola: little son, - daughter
filius: son
foraneus: non-burgher
frater: brother
fuit 36 annis: he was 36 years

G

gemelli- ae: twins

H

habitans: living
hebdomada: week
heri: yesterday

hic: here
hodie (hodiernus): today (of today)
hora: hour
huius (hujus) : of here

I

impedimentum: marriage impediment
impedimentum affinitatis: the parties are related
    by marriage
impedimentum disparitatis cultus: one is
    baptized, the other one is not
impedimentum mixtae religionis: one is baptized
    catholic, the other is baptized non-catholic
in cemeterio: in the cemetery
incerti patris: father unknown
in choro: in the church choir
incola: inhabitant
incolarum hujus: residents of this place
in doloribus partus: during child delivery
infans: infant
infrascriptus: the undersigned
iniverunt matrimonium: they married
in necessitate baptizatus: baptized in an
    emergency
innominis: without a name
in partu: during the delivery
ita est: it is thus (a declaration of authenticity)

J

Juncti sunt matrimonio: are united in marriage
J.U.L. = juris utriusque licentiatus: licentiate in
    both civil and canonical law
juvenis: young man

L

libra (lb): pound
legitimatus per subsequentem matrimonium:
    legitimized by the marriage
levantes: baptism witnesses; godparents
loco: in the place of
legitimare: legitimize

M

maiorennis: major, of age

mane: in the morning

maritata: married (for a woman)

maritus: husband (or 'married')

masculini generis: of the masculine gender

mater: mother

matrina: godmother

matrimonium contraxerunt: they married

matutinus: in the morning

media nocte: at midnight

mensis: month

meridie: at noon

meridies: south

minorrenis: minor

missa solemnis: solemn mass (for a burial)

moribundorum sacramenta: sacraments of the sick

mortuus, -a: deceased

mulier: woman

N

nativus,-a: born in

natus, -a: born

nesciens scribere: not being able to write

noctis: at night

nomen: name

nullo allato impedimento: without marriage impediment

nepos: nephew

nudius tertius: day before yesterday

nupta: wife

O

obdormivit: died

ob periculum mortis: because of danger of death

omnibus exeuntium(extremis) sacramentis: with all the sacraments of the dying

obiit: died

occidens: the west

(cum) officio novem(sex, tres) lectionum: with the singing of nine (six. three) lessons at a burial

oriens: the east

oriundus: coming from

P

parentes: parents

parochianus: parishioner

partu: during delivery

pater: father

pater ignotus: father unknown

patrinus: godfather

patruus: uncle on father's side

pbr (abbr.) presbyter: priest

p.m. (piae memoriae): of pious memory

postmeridianus: in the afternoon

posthumus: born after the death of the father

postridie: the day before yesterday

post trinam proclamationem: after three banns

praemissis proclamationibus: after the banns

praesentibus testibus: in the presence of witnesses

pridie: the day before

primogenitus, -a: the first born

priore anno: the year before

proles: child

proles spuria: illegitimate child

puer: child

Q

quod attestor, quod testor: which I confirm

R

rebaptizatus: re-baptized

registrum baptizatorum: register of the baptized

registrum matrimonio iunctorum: register of the married

registrum defunctorum: register of the dead

relicta: widow

relictus viduus: widower

S

scabinus: alderman

sepelivi: I have buried

septimana: week

sepultus, -a: buried
  "   *in ecclesia*: buried in the church
  "   *in ecclesiae navi*: buried in the nave of the
     church
  "   *in templo*: buried in the church
  "   *in choro* : buried in the choir
se scribere ignorare declaraverunt: they
     declared being unable to write
sponsa: spouse
sponsalia: engagement
spurius, spuria: illegitimate son (daughter)
status animarum: (state of the souls) a list of
     parishioners
sub conditione: under condition (used for a
     baptism performed by a lay person when a
     child was in danger of dying)
sub mediam noctem: around midnight
sub meridiem: around noon
sub vespram: by evening
susceperunt: they were godparents
susceptor,-es: godfather, - godparents
susceptrix: godmother
suscipientibus: with as godparents

T

templum: church
testes fuerunt: the witnesses were
trimestris: three months old
tumulatus: buried

U

ultima: last day of the month
ut patet in registro: as it is written in the register
uxor: wife
uxorata: a married woman
uxuratus: a married man

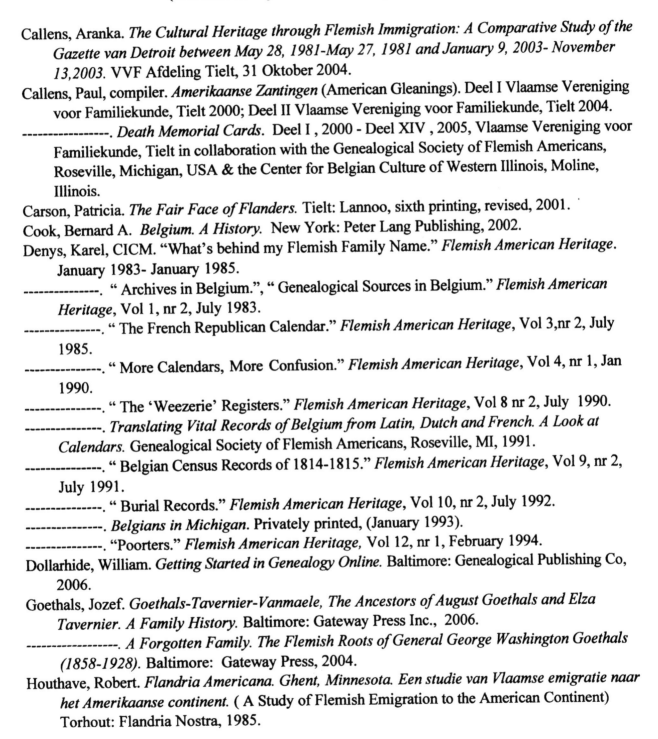

(A translation of the Flemish titles follows the source)

Callens, Aranka. *The Cultural Heritage through Flemish Immigration: A Comparative Study of the Gazette van Detroit between May 28, 1981-May 27, 1981 and January 9, 2003- November 13,2003.* VVF Afdeling Tielt, 31 Oktober 2004.

Callens, Paul, compiler. *Amerikaanse Zantingen* (American Gleanings). Deel I Vlaamse Vereniging voor Familiekunde, Tielt 2000; Deel II Vlaamse Vereniging voor Familiekunde, Tielt 2004.

------------------. *Death Memorial Cards.* Deel I , 2000 - Deel XIV , 2005, Vlaamse Vereniging voor Familiekunde, Tielt in collaboration with the Genealogical Society of Flemish Americans, Roseville, Michigan, USA & the Center for Belgian Culture of Western Illinois, Moline, Illinois.

Carson, Patricia. *The Fair Face of Flanders.* Tielt: Lannoo, sixth printing, revised, 2001.

Cook, Bernard A. *Belgium. A History.* New York: Peter Lang Publishing, 2002.

Denys, Karel, CICM. "What's behind my Flemish Family Name." *Flemish American Heritage.* January 1983- January 1985.

---------------. " Archives in Belgium.", " Genealogical Sources in Belgium." *Flemish American Heritage*, Vol 1, nr 2, July 1983.

---------------. " The French Republican Calendar." *Flemish American Heritage*, Vol 3,nr 2, July 1985.

---------------. " More Calendars, More Confusion." *Flemish American Heritage*, Vol 4, nr 1, Jan 1990.

---------------. " The 'Weezerie' Registers." *Flemish American Heritage*, Vol 8 nr 2, July 1990.

---------------. *Translating Vital Records of Belgium from Latin, Dutch and French. A Look at Calendars.* Genealogical Society of Flemish Americans, Roseville, MI, 1991.

---------------. " Belgian Census Records of 1814-1815." *Flemish American Heritage*, Vol 9, nr 2, July 1991.

---------------. " Burial Records." *Flemish American Heritage*, Vol 10, nr 2, July 1992.

---------------. *Belgians in Michigan.* Privately printed, (January 1993).

---------------. "Poorters." *Flemish American Heritage,* Vol 12, nr 1, February 1994.

Dollarhide, William. *Getting Started in Genealogy Online.* Baltimore: Genealogical Publishing Co, 2006.

Goethals, Jozef. *Goethals-Tavernier-Vanmaele, The Ancestors of August Goethals and Elza Tavernier. A Family History.* Baltimore: Gateway Press Inc., 2006.

------------------. *A Forgotten Family. The Flemish Roots of General George Washington Goethals (1858-1928).* Baltimore: Gateway Press, 2004.

Houthave, Robert. *Flandria Americana. Ghent, Minnesota. Een studie van Vlaamse emigratie naar het Amerikaanse continent.* (A Study of Flemish Emigration to the American Continent) Torhout: Flandria Nostra, 1985.

Houthave, Robert & Goddeeris, John. *Flandria Americana.* Kortemark-Handzame: Flandria et Patria, 1983.

Musschoot, Dirk. *We gaan naar Amerika, Vlaamse Landverhuizers naar de Nieuwe Wereld.* (We go to America, Flemish Emigrants to the New World) Tielt: Lannoo, 2002.

Neyt, Luc. *Cohier vander Stede van Thielt binnen vanden XXste Penning, 1571.*(Cohier of the City of inner Thielt of the XXth Penny, 1571) Tielt: VVF, 2003.

Roelstraete, Johan. *Je Stamboom, je Familiegeschiedenis, Stap voor Stap.*(Your family tree. Your family history. Step-by-step) Leuven: Davidsfonds, 2006.

--------------------. *Handleiding voor Genealogisch Onderzoek in Vlaanderen.* (Manual for Genealogical Research in Flanders). Roeselare: VVF, 1998.

Rogiers, Gilbert. *Het kasteel van Lozer. 350 jaar bezit van de familie della Faille d'Huysse.*(The Castle of Lozer. 808080350 in Possession of the Family della Faille d'Huysse) (2004).

Sabbe, Philemon D. and Buyse, Leon. *Belgians in America.* Lannoo, Tielt: Lannoo, 1960.

Vanderhaeghe, Jan. *Speuren naar je voorouders. Praktisch Stamonderzoek.*(Looking for your Ancestors. Practical Family Tree Research). VVF 1995 (2nd revised edition).

Verthé, Arthur. *150 Years of Flemings in Detroit.* Tielt: Lannoo, 1983.

Karel Denys, born in Roeselare, Belgium, 25 July 1920, joined the international missionary institute of the Immaculate Heart of Mary (CICM), at Scheut-Brussels in 1938. He was ordained a priest in 1944 and left for Peking, China, in 1947. The dangerous political situation in China caused him to be sent to the U.S.A. in 1948 where he served in parishes in northern Virginia, Philadelphia and central Louisiana. He became pastor of our Lady of Sorrows, the "Belgian Church" in Detroit in 1973. Father Denys was involved in the ethnic activities of the Flemish-American community in greater Detroit and was editor of the " Gazette van Detroit"- known as the "only Belgian Newspaper in America" - from 1982 to 1996. He also was a co-founder of the Genealogical Society of Flemish Americans. Karel presently resides at the headquarters of the CICM at Missionhurst in Arlington, Virginia, where he is archivist of the American province.

Jozef Goethals, born in Torhout, Belgium on 8 March 1937, also joined the CICM in 1956. After his studies in Nijmegen, the Netherlands, and the Gregorian University in Rome, Italy, he served as missionary in the Philippines until 1970. He emigrated to the U.S.A. that year and became a teacher in Baltimore, Maryland, where he still resides. For 32 years he taught philosophy, theology, Latin, French and Italian at Notre Dame Preparatory School and, for 8 years, Italian at the Peabody Institute of Johns Hopkins University. After his retirement in 2002 he dedicated himself entirely to his hobby: genealogy. He has published two family histories on the Goethals and self-published several genealogical reports.

A Forgotten Family. The Flemish Roots of General George Washington Goethals (1858-1928),
    Gateway Press, Inc. Baltimore MD 2004.

*Goethals-Tavernier-Vanmaele, The Ancestors of August Goethals and Elza Tavernier. A Family
    History. De Voorouders van August Goethals en Elza Tavernier. Een Familiegeschiedenis.*
    Gateway Press, Inc. Baltimore MD 2006 (published in English and Flemish).

Privately printed:

*Baptisms, Marriages and Deaths of the Goethals in selected parish records of Ghent-Belgium (1584-
    1796)*, Baltimore MD 2001.
*Debrabander. Drie eeuwen molenaars in Rumbeke en Roeselare. (Three Centuries of Millers in
    Rumbeke and Roeselare).* Baltimore MD 2002.
The Ancestors of Cardinal Godfried Danneels, Baltimore MD 2006.
*Vanhauwaert in Machelen, Olsene, Oeselgem, Vichte. The ancestors of Josephine Emelie
    Vanhauwaert (!898-1985), wife of Firmin Debrabander (1891-1958)*, Baltimore MD 2006.
The Ancestors of Father Jan Baptist Morel, CICM, Baltimore MD 2006.
*The Ancestors of Hennie Irma De Zutter. A Report on the De Zutter Family in Moerkerke,
    Lapscheure and Blankenberge since 1661.* Baltimore MD 2007.